A Creative Approach to Teaching Science Outdoors

A Creative Approach to Teaching Science Outdoors

The what, why and how of adding nature to your science lessons

Dr Penny Fletcher and Dr Sai Pathmanathan

BLOOMSBURY EDUCATION
LONDON OXFORD NEW YORK NEW DELHI SYDNEY

BLOOMSBURY EDUCATION
Bloomsbury Publishing Plc
50 Bedford Square, London, WC1B 3DP, UK
29 Earlsfort Terrace, Dublin 2, D02 AY28, Ireland
Bloomsbury Publishing Ireland Limited

BLOOMSBURY, BLOOMSBURY EDUCATION and the Diana logo are trademarks of Bloomsbury Publishing Plc

First published in Great Britain in 2025 by Bloomsbury Publishing Plc

Text copyright © Dr Penny Fletcher and Dr Sai Pathmanathan, 2025

Illustrations copyright © Jimmy Peacock, 2025; page 65, top Addinia/Shutterstock;
page 55, Shutterstock/BlueRingMediapage; page 75, r.malunki/Shutterstock, page 125, Arif_Vector/Shutterstock;
weather icon throughout, Net Vector/Shutterstock

Dr Penny Fletcher and Dr Sai Pathmanathan have asserted their rights under the Copyright, Designs
and Patents Act, 1988, to be identified as Authors of this work

Bloomsbury Publishing Plc does not have any control over, or responsibility for, any third-party websites
referred to or in this book. All internet addresses given in this book were correct at the time of going to press.
The author and publisher regret any inconvenience caused if addresses have changed or sites have
ceased to exist, but can accept no responsibility for any such changes

All rights reserved. No part of this publication may, be: i) reproduced or transmitted in any form, electronic
or mechanical, including photocopying, recording or by means of any information storage or retrieval system
without prior permission in writing from the publishers; or ii) used or reproduced in any way for the training,
development or operation of artificial intelligence (AI) technologies, including generative AI technologies.
The rights holders expressly reserve this publication from the text and data mining exception as per Article
4(3) of the Digital Single Market Directive (EU) 2019/790

A catalogue record for this book is available from the British Library

ISBN: PB: 978-1-8019-9483-5; ePDF: 978-1-8019-9486-6; ePub: 978-1-8019-9485-9

2 4 6 8 10 9 7 5 3 1

Typeset by Newgen KnowledgeWorks Pvt. Ltd., Chennai, India
Printed and bound in the UK by CPI Group (UK) Ltd., Croydon CR0 4YY

To find out more about our authors and books visit www.bloomsbury.com
and sign up for our newsletters

For product safety related questions contact: productsafety@bloomsbury.com

Acknowledgements

The authors would like to thank the following people for their feedback and advice, trialling the activities and generally amazing support: James Bamford, Tina Chawla, Theresa Crossley, Emily Huntley, Penny Kemp, Ashleigh D. Klingman, Sarah Langford, Paul McCrory, Nicola Port, Matt Pritchard and Heidi Smith.

To the great outdoors and all who are inspired by it – PF

To all the teachers who simply took us outdoors to learn something new – SP

About the authors

Dr Penny Fletcher has worked in public engagement and informal science education for over ten years. While currently the Corporate and Public Engagement Manager at the Royal College of Pathologists (RCPath), Penny's academic background (and true passion) is in ecology: Penny completed a PhD on the pollination of wild plants in arable ecosystems in 2010. During her time working on her PhD, Penny developed and delivered a range of science activities about plants, insects and ecology for children, young people and the wider public. This led to her career in science public engagement.

To date, Penny has worked on public engagement with Imperial College London, the Royal Society of Biology and the British Science Association. These roles, including her current role with RCPath, have led Penny to develop curriculum-linked science resources for teachers and engagement activities for public events such as Green Man Festival and Cheltenham Science Festival.

Penny also co-created the Little Growers Club with Dr Sai Pathmanathan. Originally an online resource, the Little Growers Club is now a gardening club for 7–11-year-olds at Streatham Common Community Garden (SCCG), thanks to a successful funding bid Sai and Penny put together in 2020. As a Trustee of SCCG, Penny facilitated outdoor learning workshops, including for a local nursery and a refugee children's group. Penny is halfway through her master's degree in Outdoor Education, which she will resume when her young son is a bit older.

Dr Sai Pathmanathan is a science education consultant with over 20 years of experience in engaging public and school audiences with diverse STEM topics. With an academic background in both neuroscience and science education, Sai understands how to help young people to engage with and understand complex STEM topics with ease. She has written a number of books and organises events, training and workshops for school-aged students, academics, teachers and the general public, often using hands-on activities, storytelling and entertainment media. She develops science education resources and runs free after-school science clubs and community workshops around the topics of food, health and the environment. Sai also consults on science communication and public-engagement projects, especially ones that promote equity, diversity and inclusion in education.

Her master's research, which looked into how young people learn accurate science from entertainment media, saw Sai take up an International Fellowship at the National Science Foundation in Washington D.C. and a Churchill Fellowship. She has held roles in science education at the Physiological Society, Nesta, Planet Science, Science in School, Ignite! and Queen Mary University of London, and has worked with many others as a consultant.

Contents

Foreword by Heidi Smith — xi

Introduction — 1

How to use this book — 3

Table of curriculum links — 8

Section 1 Science outside
Get over it — 15
Weave got strength — 17
Leaf me to race — 19
That sinking feeling — 21
Water day — 22
The heat is on — 24
Feather forecast — 26
Time for a change — 28
The big freeze — 30
Changing colours — 31
Toppling towers — 34
Sound it out — 35
Spin me right 'round — 37
Shadows and light — 39
Tendon loving care — 41
Guess who? — 42
Seeds of time — 44
Sunflower power — 47
Sum it up — 50
A-maze-ing potatoes — 52
You're the lichen to my moss — 54
Bioblitz investigation — 57

Section 2 Science games
Game-changer — 63
Making a splash — 65

Poohsticks	66
The hole illusion	68
Let's pretend	70
Remember, remember	72
What on earth?	74
Music to my ears	76
Makes a lot of scents	78
Incredible edibles	80
Seed-sational	82
Paint with nature	86

Section 3 How are we linked to nature?

Reduce; reuse; recycle	91
Berry nice	93
Bring in the bees	97
Wildlife needs you	100
Can weeds help us?	105
Plants vs. pests	108
The wonderful world of worms	111
Rain savers	114
Ice to see you	115
Tiny plastic everywhere	118
Picking straws	119
Natural manufacturing	121
Wear on Earth	123
What was here before us?	125
Audio trails	128
Circle of influence	130

Bibliography	133
Index	135
Notes	139

Foreword

Young people today live in a world that is facing biodiversity loss at a rate faster than ever before, and in a time when challenges to health and wellbeing are ever-increasing. Outdoor play and learning have consistently been shown to benefit both health and wellbeing, as well as our understanding of biodiversity and the climate crisis. Learning about the natural world through a scientific lens is essential for children so that they can, from a young age, behave in ways that will support the healing of the planet alongside other generations. It is not young people's responsibility to solve the world's environmental problems. It is, however, our obligation as educators to ensure they have the learning opportunities outdoors, indoors and online to equip them with the knowledge, skills and disposition needed to live and thrive in this world.

This book provides educators in both formal and informal settings with tangible activities to offer young people learning opportunities in and about the natural world, how it interacts with itself, and the ways in which humans impact the natural world. More importantly, it focuses on how we might live in synergy with the natural world through understanding it from a scientific perspective. The creativity offered through the activities in this book transcends what we might expect as science education. Instead, it inspires the imagination of the educator to modify what is presented in statutory curricula and, in many cases, offer interdisciplinary opportunities for learning.

It is clear these two experienced and knowledgeable educators love what they do, and I was immediately inspired by their work. Throughout this book, they invite you into their learning spaces and share a wealth of ideas and activities, all ready to be used as they are and adaptable to suit your setting and learners. This is a timely and welcome resource for educators in all settings to help us take science outside the classroom, beyond the explosions and scientific experiments we may all remember from our own schooling. What I like most about this book is the warm way in which it is written, and how that welcomes you into the ideas and activities. I trust others will experience a similar welcome and believe this will encourage all educators to pick this book up, explore the ideas found within its pages and embrace teaching science outdoors, as well as indoors and online.

Heidi Smith is a Lecturer of Outdoor Environmental Education at the University of Edinburgh. She has over 20 years of experience working in both outdoor and sustainability education, and teacher education.

Introduction

We know that being outdoors is good for us: we need sunshine for vitamin D and the trees for oxygen, and we know that being close to nature and surrounded by green helps our mental health and anxiety levels. So imagine what *learning* outdoors can do. All children, regardless of age, ability or background, respond positively in some way to being outdoors. Sometimes it's simply the extra space to waft their arms around and not having to sit down at a desk. Maybe the open air makes them feel freer to communicate their thoughts. Using the outdoors as a classroom helps children learn to love nature. When children learn to love nature, they will want to find ways to protect it too.

Sometimes, when we think about teaching and learning outdoors, a lesson becomes solely about wildlife and survival skills – a science lesson without being called science. While these skills are great and useful, they aren't the only topics that can be taught outdoors. What about the curriculum we can teach outside with *whatever* is found outdoors? We could look at floating and sinking in rainwater butts, or building structures out of twigs to study forces. Adapting our 'typical' science activities to be run outside gives children the chance to play and appreciate the outdoors, and us educators (whether in school or at home) to make the most of our outdoor spaces and natural resources while still delivering the curriculum. This is something we've been experimenting with. It's why we wrote this book.

A Creative Approach to Teaching Science Outdoors is an environmentally friendly guide for all educators of 5–11-year-olds who wish to take practical science outside and show children that science is truly everywhere. It builds on what the children have learned in their early education, and contains a mixture of hands-on and curriculum-linked activities, games and investigations. There are projects encouraging local community engagement and cultural relevancy, all linked to science curricula across the UK. With minor adaptations (mentioned where applicable), most of these activities can easily be run with younger children. Some activities could also be called STEAM (science, technology, engineering, arts and mathematics). All of the activities have various cross-curricular links and are inherently creative, because *scientists are creative*.

The overarching theme of the book is inspired by Dr Matt Pritchard's 'learning cycle of wonder' and finding the '"Wow! How? Now…?"' in the science around us (Pritchard, 2018). For example, we may be in awe of a cloud, learn about the water cycle and then we're even more in awe. Learning the 'how' then encourages the 'What if?' stage, which leads to new discoveries. By starting with the natural world around us we have so many opportunities to engage children in science outside of the typical explosions and 'magic potions' (though we can find natural examples of these outdoors too).

As Dr Paul McCrory says in *Hook Your Audience* (2021), 'a hook is any stimulus that provokes the involuntary attention of all your learners' (p.12). As educators, we can take advantage of children's increased curiosity and heightened state of alertness when they're outdoors to gain this involuntary attention. The novelty can be overwhelming and children may get distracted by all the extra stimuli at first. Giving them time to play, explore and ask questions can ease them into this new learning environment and help us better understand what interests them. Going outside every lesson will eventually make the environment less exciting, but doing outdoor work regularly in a few local spaces will allow you to continue getting the benefits. This creates an engaging atmosphere for learning in a much easier, cheaper and more manageable way than, for example, taking children on class trips to highly stimulating environments.

We also know we need to support children with their mental health and reduce levels of Nature-Deficit Disorder, a term coined by Richard Louv (2005). He described how many of us, including children, spend too much time indoors and not enough time in nature. This can lead to negative moods, behavioural issues and reduced attention spans. Being outdoors is extremely calming and engaging for all, but especially for children with special educational needs and disabilities (SEND). Being outdoors can make many young people feel more positive and at ease with learning, especially those who struggle with writing and literacy or use English as an additional language (EAL).

Not only are the activities in this book based outdoors for these reasons, but they have also been designed to be low cost, environmentally friendly, playful, exciting and engaging, supporting children to develop a variety of skills useful for being not only future scientists, but also future citizens. The activities are also ideal for home-schooling, forest schools, science weeks, science fairs, homework tasks, project-based learning, science clubs, Rainbows, Brownies, Beavers, Cubs and other after-school groups. The activities have links to other curriculum areas to help children make connections with their science knowledge, thereby adding to their science capital. (Science capital is how much a person feels connected to and values science based on an accumulation of their science-related experiences, understanding, attitudes, knowledge, interests and of the people they know in science-related careers.)

This book aims to make adapting our current curriculum to the outdoors – and its benefits – as accessible as possible. We encourage the use of easily accessible, naturally available and environmentally friendly materials. Plenty of adaptations are provided, depending on whether you're in a rural or an urban environment, so no one misses out on any of the outdoor fun. Use these activities to support every child's wellbeing, and their love of science, nature and community. We hope that the fun, practical and engaging activities in this book bring you and your groups as much joy as it did in our workshops. We can't wait to hear what you think!

Penny and Sai

How to use this book

There are three sections in the book, each containing a set of activities based around a different theme. The activities are designed to be around 30–40 minutes long but can be shortened to starters or expanded to a sequence of investigations, depending on the ages and interests of the group you are working with. See the table of curriculum links on pages 8–11, which shows the links between each activity and the statutory subjects for each devolved nation, as well as cross-curricular links where relevant. Additional resources, templates and links are also available on the book's companion website at www.saipathmanathan.com/ScienceOutdoors.

Section 1: Science outside

This section contains activities that are closely curriculum based. These activities feature ways to take common science lessons outdoors, rather than running them as desk-based or indoor activities. In this way, children will understand that science learning can truly take place anywhere, not just in the classroom.

Section 2: Science games

This section contains activities that are more play based, while stealthily taking the curriculum learning further. This is where children get to see the fun side of science learning, which isn't just about watching explosions or making 'potions'. These activities contain games, puzzles and illusions with suggestions for how to incorporate both high- and low-tech ideas into whatever outdoor space you may have. This section engages children in science in a playful way, while still being just as grounded in rigorous scientific methods and concepts.

Section 3: How are we linked to nature?

This section contains some familiar outdoor activities but takes the applying, thinking and discussion a step further. It brings in cross-curricular elements, such as using crafts, to help discuss the environment and our place in nature. Each activity includes discussion prompts and scientific demonstrations for children to think more widely about climate and environmental issues, as well as providing small positive steps to impact their future.

Running the activities

Some activities work extremely well together and can be built into a lesson sequence over a period of a few weeks. For example, 'Sound it out', 'Music to my ears' and 'Audio trails' are all to do with sound and would work well as a sequence of lessons across a couple of weeks. Alternatively, complementary activities can be used to revisit the same topic at different times during the school year. Some activities use similar materials or cover the same environmental messages, and these ideas are included in each activity. Do encourage children to see the connections between activities so that they start to question and hypothesise, allowing you to plan ways to take their ideas and experiments further.

The main task for each activity can be run with all children, regardless of age group. Children in Upper Key Stage 2 will benefit from the 'Further investigation' tasks. Children with special educational needs may need additional support in some activities, as could those with physical disabilities (such as in the 'Tendon loving care' activity). Those with EAL will be at ease with practical activities (as most do not require any writing), but they can be encouraged to communicate verbally to practise language skills and to learn scientific vocabulary alongside their peers. As the instructions are easy to follow and all materials are safe, light and natural, the activities are inclusive.

Some activities are more suitable for warm temperatures and others for cold, or for some parts of the year more than others, in which case you'll see this weather icon in the margin. However, all activities can be adapted to the different seasons, including by going indoors where necessary – though being outside allows for much messier activities!

Safety notes

While we have offered various options and alternatives within each activity, you will know what suits your group best, so do adapt the activities and materials accordingly.

Allergies

You will already be aware of your group's allergies and sensitivities, especially around hay fever at certain times of year. Some children may have allergies to different pollens or have sensitivities to plants (such as seeds, herbs or leaves like nettles) that they are not aware of, which will be important to watch out for when they are searching for specimens outdoors. For example, weeds such as dandelions are generally considered safe; however, the sap from the stalks is a type of latex, which might cause skin irritations. Other leaves and plants may be sharp (such as cordyline, courgette stalks and rose thorns), so we recommend having gloves and a first-aid kit on hand. Check the Royal Horticultural Society website for a list of potentially harmful plants so you can keep an eye out for them.

Note Pages

We have added extra blank pages at the back of this book. You might find these helpful for jotting down ideas or useful websites, or to sketch diagrams for your class, for example, how to illustrate a minibeast or trace around a shadow. This may save you from chasing after sheets of paper blowing around outdoors!

Weather

As with all outdoor activities in exposed areas without shade, do make sure children wear hats and sunscreen (with a high SPF) and provide plenty of drinking water for hydration, especially if running any of these activities during the peak sunshine in the summer term. While being in the sunshine is great for boosting vitamin D levels and improves our eyesight (so long as we're not focused on simply what's near to our eyes, such as books and screens), do make sure children don't look directly at the Sun. Winter coats, gloves and waterproof clothing may be needed for activities during the colder months, such as when working with rainwater, puddles, snow and ice.

Limited outdoor space

Of course, there are many schools (especially in inner cities) where there is extremely limited outdoor space. We have given options in the activities to help encourage outdoor learning whatever the area, though it may be possible to run some activities indoors. Perhaps add to the novelty by making sure it is a fully practical session and in a new area for the children (i.e. not in their regular classroom).

Being environmentally friendly and using what you have

Task the children to make use of what they can find. We have provided options of various items, but it's completely up to you and your group to find what will work based on where you are and the season you are working in.

To prevent waste and to encourage the use of what is available on our doorsteps, why not collect rainwater for water-based activities? Try growing plants throughout the year: there are several bulbs that will pop up at different times of the year (e.g. daffodils, alliums, gladioli and snowdrops), which can be easily grown in pots with minimal resources and effort. Other plants that are easy to grow from seed include mint, nasturtium and basil. With careful planning, many of these activities could even be completely zero-waste, with all items being composted and adding nutrients back into the soil.

Aim to limit food waste as much as possible, asking children and other staff members to bring in their unused items and food scraps from home as relevant. If food needs to be thrown away, add it to compost. (You could start a compost bin at your school if there isn't one already.)

This book aims to be as environmentally friendly and accessible as possible, and it is always best to use what you have rather than buying more. We have avoided recommending single-use plastic items in the activities; however, plastic items are sometimes required where other materials are not suitable (e.g. waterproofing for animal habitats). In these cases, we recommend using any reusable or recyclable plastic you may have. When you do need to buy items to use in these activities, aim for items packaged in glass, paper or cardboard, which can all be recycled.

Please see a list of common items in the activities, with guidance on finding readily available eco-alternatives.

Eco washing-up liquid	This is best sourced from environmental companies creating packaging that is recyclable or biodegradable or use cruelty-free, non-animal-derivative bars of soap in cardboard boxes, which can be recycled or composted.
Collected rainwater	Rather than always using water from the tap, aim to collect rainwater on site using a water butt throughout the year. Save any unused water at the ends of activities for painting, watering plants or cleaning and mopping the floor rather than pouring it down the sink.
Recycled paper tape	No glue or sticky tape is used in the activities, as these tend not to be good for the environment. Aim for recycled paper tape where needed.
Recycled plant pots	Use recycled plastic pots, such as yoghurt pots or homemade planters from recycled cardboard (as in 'Making recycled plant pots' on page 45), or plastic plant pots if you already own them.
Peat-free compost	You can use soil from outdoors, a mix of soil and top soil or compost for these activities. If soil isn't available in your setting, local garden centres, community gardens and allotments may be able to provide top soil and even homemade compost. When purchasing small bags of compost, peat-free compost is better for the environment (as the excessive mining of peat bogs has destroyed many habitats, threatening many species of wildlife). Compost bags are useful for repurposing too, such as for planting potatoes. If there is no outdoor space for growing, the activities can also be completed in pots and planters.
Natural items	For every activity that includes a variety of natural items, these can be collected by you or the children at the start of your session – whatever works best for your group. Children shouldn't strip the environment of all foliage while carrying out these activities, so reuse wherever possible. If unavailable in your outdoor spaces, some items may be borrowed from friendly local allotments and neighbours, or purchased at minimal expense. Some garden centres offer vouchers or are happy to donate seeds and plants.

You may need to use technology outdoors, such as tablets, mobile phones, digital microscopes and data loggers wherever mentioned. Make sure children are careful not to drop these on hard surfaces or into water. When observing nature in early-education settings, children might want to 'take a photo with their eyes'. Children can act as if they are holding cameras up, and click the shutter by making a pretend 'click' noise. You can then ask them to 'file' those images in their brains for later. These kinaesthetic actions help children to catch their moments of learning.

Thinking like scientists

Encourage children to hypothesise, think about what could happen, make predictions, use their senses, observe closely and wonder 'What if?'. Do children understand the concept of a fair test, do their ideas need testing further, and can they repeat their tests to prove their results are not simply one-offs? Children can record their results, but rather than taking worksheets and stationery outside (which fly away on windy days), why not use chalk on the ground or a board instead? Each activity has the option to carry out further investigations in the setting or at home, enabling those children interested in science to take their learning further. You could even encourage children to take part in science-festival events and awards, such as the British Science Association's CREST Awards.

As children are expected to think and work scientifically – understanding how science works as well as developing transferable skills, such as communication, numeracy and listening skills – we have included a vast array of tasks within each activity that assist with nurturing this. Through these enjoyable and creative activities, children will be more able to spot patterns, understand the concept of a fair test, learn how to identify and classify, understand what it means to investigate and experiment, and much more.

Teaching diversity natives

> 'We call [young people] digital natives but they're also diversity natives. They've never known any society that didn't look like the one that we live in today.'
>
> David Olusoga, Children's Media Conference 2023

Many children in classrooms all over the country have diverse backgrounds and have travelled to exciting places around the globe, experiencing the natural world in ways many of we adults can only imagine. Take the time to connect children's cultural experiences to the activities. Let their understanding shape activities, such as around using natural materials instead of plastics, sustainable fashion and growing different plants for food.

Table of curriculum links

Chapter	Activity	Plants	Animals, including humans	Everyday materials (uses, properties and changes)	Seasonal changes	Living things and their habitats	Rocks	Light	Forces and magnets	States of matter	Sound	Electricity	Earth and space	Evolution and inheritance
Section 1 Science outside	Get over it			x					x					
	Weave got strength	x		x					x					
	Leaf me to race			x					x					
	That sinking feeling						x		x	x				
	Water day	x				x			x					
	The heat is on				x			x		x			x	
	Feather forecast		x	x		x								
	Time for a change		x	x			x			x				
	The big freeze				x					x				
	Changing colours	x		x			x							
	Toppling towers						x		x					
	Sound it out		x			x					x			
	Spin me right 'round	x							x					
	Shadows and light	x						x						
	Tendon loving care		x			x								
	Guess who?	x	x			x	x							
	Sunflower power	x	x		x	x								
	Seeds of time	x				x								
	Sum it up	x				x								
	A-maze-ing potatoes	x					x							
	You're the lichen to my moss	x			x	x	x							x
	Bioblitz investigation	x	x			x								

8   A Creative Approach to Teaching Science Outdoors

Northern Ireland Foundation to Primary 7 'The World Around Us'				Scotland Primary 2 to 7 Sciences					Wales Foundation to Key Stage 2 Science			Other curriculum areas								
Interdependence	Place	Movement and energy	Change over time	Planet Earth	Forces, electricity and waves	Biological systems	Materials	Topical science	Interdependence	The sustainable Earth	How things work	Language, literacy and drama	Mathematics and numeracy	Art	PE, PSHE and wellbeing	Design and technology	Music	Geography, history and social studies	Computing	Careers and the world of work
		X			X		X				X	X				X				X
X		X			X		X			X	X				X			X		
		X			X						X									
		X			X		X				X									
X	X			X					X	X									X	
X		X	X	X				X	X	X								X		
	X	X	X	X		X	X		X	X				X				X	X	
			X				X			X								X		
			X	X				X		X									X	
X			X	X			X		X						X			X		
		X	X		X														X	
	X	X			X						X					X		X		
X		X			X				X		X							X		
X		X	X	X	X				X		X				X			X		X
	X	X				X					X					X				
X	X			X					X	X					X			X		X
X	X		X	X					X	X				X					X	
X	X		X	X					X	X									X	
X			X	X					X	X			X							X
X									X									X		
X	X	X	X	X					X	X					X			X		
X	X		X	X					X	X			X						X	

Table of curriculum links

		England Key Stages 1 and 2 Science										
Section 2 Science games	Game-changer		x					x				
	Making a splash		x					x	x			
	Poohsticks							x				
	The hole illusion		x				x					
	Let's pretend					x		x					
	Remember, remember		x			x						
	What on earth?					x	x					
	Music to my ears			x				x		x		
	Makes a lot of scents	x	x									
	Incredible edibles	x	x									
	Seed-sational	x		x								
	Paint with nature	x	x	x		x						
Section 3 How are we linked to nature?	Reduce; reuse; recycle			x								
	Berry nice	x	x			x						
	Bring in the bees		x			x				x		x
	Wildlife needs you		x	x		x						
	Can weeds help us?	x	x		x	x						
	Plants vs. pests	x	x			x						
	The wonderful world of worms		x			x	x					
	Rain savers	x				x			x			
	Ice to see you				x				x			
	Tiny plastic everywhere		x	x		x						
	Picking straws	x										
	Natural manufacturing	x		x			x					
	Wear on earth	x		x								
	What was here before us?	x	x			x	x					x
	Audio trails		x			x				x		
	Circle of influence		x		x	x						x

10   A Creative Approach to Teaching Science Outdoors

Northern Ireland Foundation to Primary 7 'The World Around Us'				Scotland Primary 2 to 7 Sciences				Wales Foundation to Key Stage 2 Science			Other curriculum areas							
		x		x		x							x	x		x		x
				x					x									
		x		x					x	x			x					
x	x	x		x	x			x		x		x						
	x	x	x	x	x			x		x	x	x	x	x			x	x
	x			x					x		x		x					x
	x		x	x				x	x			x						
		x		x					x						x			
x	x			x		x		x										
x	x	x		x		x		x		x			x		x			
x				x			x	x	x	x			x		x			
x	x		x	x			x		x				x		x			
			x	x				x	x	x					x			
x				x		x		x	x	x					x			
x	x			x				x	x	x				x	x			
x	x		x	x				x	x	x					x			
x	x		x	x				x	x	x								
x	x		x	x				x	x	x								
x	x	x	x	x		x		x	x									
x	x		x	x				x	x									
		x		x	x			x		x						x		
x	x		x	x				x	x	x	x			x				
x								x	x	x						x		x
					x	x			x		x	x		x				x
x					x	x	x	x			x	x		x				x
x	x	x	x	x				x	x	x		x		x		x	x	
	x	x	x	x	x			x	x		x	x				x	x	x
x	x		x	x			x	x	x	x		x		x		x		x

Table of curriculum links 11

Section 1

Science outside

Get over it

Build bridges from natural materials in this session to introduce children to Newton's Third Law of Motion.

> **Links to other activities:** This activity works well with 'Wear on Earth', 'Weave got strength' and 'Natural manufacturing' as children will have the opportunity to think about the different types, uses and strengths of natural materials.

Materials

- A variety of cord-like natural materials, such as:
  - Twigs and branches
  - Grasses
  - Bamboo
  - Dried grasses
  - Long sturdy stems and stalks (such as from lavender, daffodils, tulips and sunflowers once they've died down)
  - Bark
  - Soil
  - Runners of weeds (such as bindweed and cinquefoils)
- Bricks, small boxes or jam jars
- A weight, such as a rock or tin of beans

> **Safety note**
> Dried cordyline leaves are strong, but might be too spiky or sharp for small hands.

Activity

Ask the children to think about any bridges they've travelled across: they could be large, which their family has driven across, or small, such as one used to walk over a babbling brook. Either way, the bridge has to support a certain amount of weight, so it must be made of strong materials.

Building a bridge

Show the children a variety of natural objects, such as twigs and branches, grasses and stems. What do they think about them? How strong are they? The children can try to snap small twigs, or tear grasses. Some of these items might be weak by themselves, but what if they were put together?

The children can work in groups or pairs. Set up two strong items, such as bricks, boxes or jars, with some distance in between (around 30–50 cm). Ask the children to find enough materials to build a bridge between those two points. The bridge must be strong enough to hold a particular weight, such as a tin of beans. You could have one brick set up ready, so the children can take turns to test their bridges and then return to the drawing board to improve their designs.

Ideas and design

Depending on your group, you may need to give the children a little guidance. For example, could several twigs be laid flat and woven or tied with grasses to create a sturdy platform between the two bricks? Could several tall grasses be plaited or woven together to create a set of ropes between the bricks, held down with large rocks or stones at either end? What plants are made of strong natural materials (like tree bark, bamboo stems and various evergreen leaves)? Could some wet soil be applied to the objects to stick them together and left to dry until hardened? Once the children are happy with their bridge designs, ask each group or pair to set their bridge up for the ultimate test… Does the bridge support the weight of the tin?

What the children will see

Bridges are structures that help us get across obstacles such as rivers, roads or railway tracks. Effective bridge-building, to keep us safe as we walk or drive along a bridge, is all down to physics and engineering.

Explain that bridge activities like this can help us understand Newton's Third Law of Motion: for every action there is an equal and opposite reaction. So the tin of beans is applying a force on the bridge (weight) and the bridge applies an equal force back on the tin of beans (tension). This is the only way the tin stays on the bridge.

Further ideas for investigation

Based on the bridges they have already made, how would the children go about improving them? They might like to make longer bridges and see if the tin of beans can be rolled along the bridges without the bridges breaking.

Triangles are one of the strongest straight-edged shapes, which is why many bridges use this shape as their building blocks in construction. Can the children find a way to make strong triangles with their natural materials? They could try placing twigs in a triangle formation and tying them at the corners with tough grasses or stems. Is it possible to make a triangle-based structure that doesn't collapse?

Weave got strength

Investigate how to make the strongest natural rope using grasses, by experimenting to lift small natural objects and playing tug of war.

> **Links to other activities:** The following activities also use natural materials, so you might want to run them in a similar time period (e.g. during a Science Week), so the children get to use all of their favourite collected materials: 'Wear on earth', 'Picking straws', 'Get over it' and 'Natural manufacturing'.

Materials

- Different types of vegetation that have long-enough leaves or stems to be woven, such as:
  - Grasses
  - Nettles (dried out in advance – see 'Making nettle cordage', page 18)
  - Wildflowers with long stems
  - Grape vines
  - Palm leaves
  - Seaweed
- Items to test strength of plant-based ropes (e.g. conkers, stones, rocks or small weights)

Section 1: Science outside

Activity

This activity is best carried out in late summer or early autumn when grass is longer and the plant material is more fibrous, and when fewer species are relying on plants for food and habitat.

If your setting has a field or is near a nature reserve, you could start this activity by challenging the children to search for long pieces of grass and vegetation. Tell them that they're going to test out the strength of different plant stems and leaves by making ropes and using them to lift things. As they collect different plant material to make their ropes, ask them to write down words that describe the feel of the different parts of the plants. It is also an opportunity to ask them if they know the names of common wild plants and for peer learning about local plant life.

If you don't have much plant life in your playground or schoolyard, or if you have only a short session for this activity, you can collect plant material such as the types listed above from any park or garden in advance of the rope-making session. If possible, dry out nettle stems in advance (as in 'Making nettle cordage' below) so the children can try using these very strong stems and compare them with other plant stems and other material.

Making nettle cordage

Materials:

- Tall nettles
- Thick gloves

Method:

1. Cut nettles at the base.
2. Remove the leaves by firmly and swiftly running your hand towards the top of the nettle, taking the weaker tip off as you go. You will be left with a smooth, bald nettle stem.
3. Remove any root or soft stem at the top and bottom of the nettle.
4. Crush the stem slightly flat.
5. Split the stem open using your fingernail or a small knife.
6. Bend the nettle stem over your index finger so that the woody, inner stem snaps outwards.
7. Remove the inner stem and air dry it. Repeat this with as many nettles as you can.

Encourage the children to think about how to make the strongest natural rope or string. Ask them to try plaiting or twisting more than one strand of plant material together. Give them a set amount of time to make their plant ropes (perhaps in teams, with each team using a different plant material) and then move on to strength tests.

Ask the children how they will design a fair test to find out which is the strongest plant rope. How will they decide to attach the rope to their weight? Encourage them to measure and write down the weight of each object before they test if their rope can lift it. If using standardised classroom weights, simply ask the children to write down each weight they're testing in turn and record what happens.

Talk about why certain parts of the plant might be stronger than others. Why do plants need to have strength? Which parts of plants might be the strongest? Stems are likely to be the strongest parts because they often contain a special material called lignin in their cell walls, which helps them do their job of carrying water and nutrients from the roots up to the leaves.

Further ideas for investigation

If you live by the sea, why not try drying out seaweed and investigating ways to make cordage or rope out of it? If you have more time (e.g. non-curriculum time during Science Week), you could challenge the children to make nets out of their plant ropes for lifting objects in the strength test. The children could also have competitions to plait the longest natural rope. They could also investigate which everyday objects are made of plants, such as paper, cotton clothing, bamboo socks and wooden furniture, and what qualities these natural materials have to make them suitable.

Leaf me to race

Using the power of surface tension, the children can race a leaf in this activity while learning about the amazing properties of water.

> **Links to other activities:** This activity works well with 'Making a Splash', 'Game-changer' and 'Poohsticks' because of the links to water's properties, such as surface tension. 'Paint with nature' uses natural inks and dyes, which the children might want to experiment with here too.

Materials

Required:

- Access to puddles or a basin of rainwater
- A variety of leaves
- Food colouring, natural ink or eco washing-up liquid
- Paintbrushes or pipettes (or children's fingers)

Optional

- Ivy leaves
- Conkers
- A pestle and mortar or secateurs and a hammer (for grown-up use only)

Activity

Start off by asking the children if they've ever seen insects walking around on a pond. Perhaps they've seen a pond skater before, or a little insect that is struggling on the surface but doesn't actually drown and sink. Explain that this is because of water's surface tension, a force that pulls the water molecules together. It's as though there is an invisible skin on the water, as water molecules are attracted to each other like tiny magnets. Some insects can travel on this surface and so can leaf boats.

Making a leaf racer

Make sure the puddle or basin of water has settled so that the surface is calm. The children can have a look at the selection of leaves or go and find their own. Which ones do they think will work best as fast boats: dry, small, large, wide, thin or pointy leaves? Ask the children to take a leaf and add a small droplet of 'fuel' (food colouring, ink or eco washing-up liquid) to one tip of the leaf using their finger, a paintbrush or a pipette. The children 'race' their leaves by placing the leaves flat on the surface of the water and then they watch them go!

The children could race against each other or take it in turns to place their leaves in the water. They could place their leaves on the water first and then simultaneously add a droplet of their chosen fuel to the ends of their leaves.

> **Teacher tip**
>
> You may need to change the water (or find another puddle) after a while, especially if the children's leaf boats don't move at all.

What the children will see

The children will see their leaves zoom around in the water, leaving colourful trails behind. Explain that the fuel spreads out from the leaf tip onto the surface of the water, forming a thin film. This reduces the water's surface tension. The water at the tip of the leaf, where the fuel was added, now has a low surface tension, while the water around the rest of the leaf has a high surface tension. Where the water has a high surface tension, the water molecules are pulled more strongly together than where the water has a low surface tension. This results in the water under the leaf getting dragged forwards, and so the leaf whooshes forwards. This is known as the Marangoni effect.

When the children dip their fingers into some food colouring or ink, they will notice it forms perfect droplets on their fingertips. This is also because of water's surface tension (explored in more detail in 'Making a splash').

Further ideas for investigation

Ask the children which leaves made the best boats. They may have naturally picked a leaf that is more boat-shaped (i.e. elliptical or lanceolate in shape), but do they think a more oval or wider cordate-type leaf would race better or worse? Perhaps they'd like to test their predictions out. Can they choose a leaf with a more streamlined shape, which would create less friction between the surface of the leaf and the water (reducing drag)?

Using a pestle and mortar or a hammer and secateurs, crush some ivy leaves or conkers for the children and ask the children to mix these with a little water. Some children may be sensitive to ivy leaves, so feel free to use conkers only. The children can try using this mix as fuel instead. What do they notice?

Both ivy leaves and conkers contain saponins (soap compounds), which behave in the same way as the other 'fuels' and lower the surface tension of the water. Another method to make leaf boats move is to dip a thin slice of the white fleshy part from inside a conker into the water right near the floating leaf.

That sinking feeling

Set up an experiment using natural objects and tubs of water to generate discussions about the properties of different materials and to introduce the concept of density.

> **Links to other activities:** You may wish to run this activity alongside other water-based activities, such as 'Leaf me to race', 'Poohsticks', 'Ice to see you' and 'Rain savers'.

Materials

Required:

- A variety of small natural items ensuring a wide range of weights so both sinking and floating can be observed (e.g. feathers, both green and dry leaves, stones, sticks, flowers, eggshells, bark, pine cones, seeds, rosehips, berries, clay and soil)
- Exercise books and pencils
- Collected rainwater
- Wide containers such as clean, empty ice-cream tubs, small metal buckets or plant pots (without holes) – one between a group of four

Optional:

- Clay

Section 1: Science outside

Activity

Either collect natural objects in advance or ask the children to spend 15 minutes at the start of the session collecting interesting objects. Then ask them to get into groups of four, with each group gathering around each container.

Ask the children to write down each of the objects they have collected and to make predictions about which of the objects will sink and which will float. They can then start to test the objects in turn, placing them in wide containers of collected rainwater, one at a time. The children should note down if their predictions were correct. Discuss why some objects float and some sink; encourage the children to talk about heavy vs. light materials.

Depending on the age of the children, you might introduce the word 'density' and ask the children to think about how tightly packed molecules are in different objects. Explain that, if an item is heavy for its size (e.g. a stone), this means its molecules are more tightly packed than water's molecules – it is denser than water so it will sink. If an item is light for its size (e.g. a feather) it has more-loosely packed molecules than water, so it will float.

Further ideas for investigation

Encourage the children to experiment with making floating objects sink by piling different items on top of them. For example, how many pieces of bark or seeds can they place on a large leaf floating on a bowl of water before it sinks?

You could also talk about or try changing the shape of a sinking object to make it float. For example, if you live in an area with lots of clay in the soil, why not try out flattening lumps of clay into thin discs to see if you can make them float?

Water day

 This set of activities offers the children a few different ways to investigate evaporation and the water cycle, and how they relate to plants. These activities work best in spring and summer.

> **Links to other activities:** 'Rain savers' works well alongside this activity.

Materials

- Glass jars with lids
- Collected rainwater
- Mobile phones, tablets, cameras or video cameras for taking photographs/filming
- Potted plants or a bed of soil with established plants (of any type)
- Small watering cans or similar

Activity

Understanding evaporation

Ask the children if they have noticed what happens to raindrops on a window once the Sun comes out – they get smaller and eventually disappear. This is because of evaporation. Heat energy from the Sun causes water to change from its liquid form to a gas called water vapour. Tell the children that today they're going to watch evaporation happen. They are also going to find out what can make evaporation speed up or slow down.

Ask the children to set up a few jar lids in a sunny spot with a coin-sized drop of water in each, and to set some others up in a shaded spot. (Somewhere north-facing should stay shady for most of the day.)

Return to the lids later in the day and encourage the children to make observations about how much smaller the drop of water is in each lid. Is there a difference between the water drops that have been in the Sun compared to those in the shade? (Some of the water drops might have disappeared altogether.) Discuss with the children why those in the Sun might have evaporated more quickly: the heat energy from the Sun caused more of the water to turn to water vapour.

If possible, set up a mobile phone (or a video camera, if you prefer) so it is filming or creating a time-lapse video of the jar lids at the start of the experiment. Later or the next day, you can show the children this sped-up version so they can see evaporation in action.

Evaporation and plants

This activity leads nicely to learning about how the water cycle links to plant growth and how best to water plants in the garden. On a sunny day, take the children out to water some potted plants or a border of plants. Ask them to work in pairs (or small groups if you have a limited number of plants to work with) to fill up watering cans and then go and water a plant. Once they have emptied their small watering cans onto their plants, ask them to describe where they can see and feel the water. They should be able to see some droplets of water on the leaves (and flowers if applicable) and they should be able to feel the water making the soil around the plant damp.

Return to the plants later in the day and observe the same areas. Are there fewer or smaller droplets of water on the leaves? Is the soil still damp? Any changes will be a result of evaporation. You can remind children about the heat energy of the Sun causing the liquid water they put on their plants to turn into a gas called water vapour. The children can think about how best to water plants in the future: plants need to absorb water from their roots, which are under the soil, and evaporation is slower from the soil than from the surfaces of leaves. So, plants will be able to use more of the water if you pour it from a watering can just onto the soil around the plant, and not onto the leaves.

Further ideas for investigation

You could investigate how best to water plants by running an experiment to compare what happens to plants that are given no water with those that are given increasing amounts of water. Give some plants very large amounts to show how over-watering can prevent plants from growing properly – they will often have yellow leaves and look 'unwell'.

On a rainy day, you could run a competition. Give each child a jar with their name on and challenge them to place it outside in a spot where they think they will collect the most rainwater. Collect the jars later in the day or the next day. Ideally, some children will have been able to place their jars under trees so you can discuss how trees might shelter the jars from the rain but how the rain might also run off the trees' leaves into the jars. This can lead to discussions about how rainwater reaches the roots of trees when they have lots of leaves.

The heat is on

Help the children better understand heat and light energy, and how we can use heat from the Sun to melt familiar foods. This activity is best carried out on a bright, sunny day.

> **Links to other activities:** The following activities also discuss heat, melting, composting and insulation: 'Time for a change', 'Feather forecast' and 'Reduce; reuse; recycle'.

Materials

Required:

- Crackers or biscuits, such as digestives
- Chocolate, cheese or butter (cut into small pieces)

24   A Creative Approach to Teaching Science Outdoors

Optional:

- Ice cubes
- Aluminium pie cases or squares of foil (roughly 10 x 10 cm)
- Different types of chocolate and cheese (white, milk and dark chocolate, and hard and soft cheese)
- Grass clippings in a box
- Trays
- Thermometers

> **Safety note**
>
> As this is an activity with food in it, make sure the children have washed their hands before they eat anything, especially if they have been handling anything outdoors. It's best not to eat anything that has been in grass clippings or compost, unless you can be sure the food has not touched the decomposing materials.

Activity

What do the children think of the sunshine? Do they enjoy being out in the Sun and playing outdoors? They will most probably all say yes. But do they ever think about the energy of the Sun? Explain that we get light and heat energy from the Sun. Ask the children: how can we use the heat energy from the Sun?

Melty snacks

We can use the heat of the Sun to melt ingredients. It's not quite cooking, but it'll still result in a delicious treat. Ask the children to take a biscuit and place a piece of chocolate on top (for a sweet snack) or take a cracker and place a knob of butter or a piece of cheese on top (for savoury). Hold the ingredients out in the Sun – the children can hold these in their hands, or place them on trays, to make sure their treats are in direct, maximum sunlight and they don't have to sit for too long in the heat. What do the children notice about the sizes of the pieces and how quickly or slowly they melt?

What the children will see

The children can check on their biscuits to see what's happening. They should notice the butter and chocolate melting. The cheese might not melt as much as it would on a grill, but will become soft, oily and slightly squishy. Ask the children to describe what they see.

Explain that chocolate is solid at room temperature, which is around 20 degrees Celsius. Any temperature above that will mean that the chocolate will start to melt. Hot sunny days in the UK can now get to above 40 degrees Celsius. The heat from the midday sun is so strong in some areas of the world, especially near the Equator, that you could melt a cheese sandwich just by leaving it outdoors.

Alternatively, the children could use ice cubes to see melting in action, or even watch a piece of chocolate melt and slide down some aluminium foil on an inclined surface.

Further ideas for investigation

Find out if the children think there is a way to collect as much of the Sun's heat as possible to melt chocolate. Ask them what they understand about conductors of heat. Explain that conductors of heat include metals, and this is why many of our cooking pans are made of aluminium, stainless steel or even copper.

By using some pieces of aluminium foil or pie dishes, the children can create an experiment to find out whether chocolate left outside on a sunny day melts more quickly on aluminium. They can investigate these questions: does chocolate melt more quickly under the shade of a tree? Do different types of chocolate (milk, dark and white) or cheese (hard and soft) melt more quickly? With or without aluminium? How do the children ensure a fair test? Should they compare the same amounts of chocolate in the same set-up – or, if comparing heat, do they keep one set inside, record the temperatures and time the melting? Encourage them to make choices to set up their own experiments, following the principles of a fair test.

If your school or local park has mowed lawns and you are able to collect the grass clippings, or if you have compost on site, another interesting investigation can be set up. As microorganisms start to break down (decompose) the plant materials, a lot of heat is generated. If the children place an aluminium dish with some chocolate on it on top of the grass clippings, what do they see? Can they measure the temperature inside and outside the grass clippings box too?

Feather forecast

Investigate how well different materials insulate. This activity combines physics and biology to help the children learn about nest-building.

> **Links to other activities:** The following activities cover heat, insulation, and how composting and biodegradation works: 'The heat is on', 'Wildlife needs you' and 'Reduce; reuse; recycle'.

Materials

Required:

- Cardboard shoe boxes or several similarly sized boxes (ideally with lids)
- Thermometers (one per box is ideal)
- Natural materials that could be used as insulation, e.g. feathers, dried leaves, moss, turf, Old Man's Beard, sheep's wool
- Access to an outdoor shed or similar dry sheltered area (for storing the nests)

Optional:

- Printed photos of birds' nests, showing insulation material
- A temperature-tracking chart

Activity

Introductory discussion

If you can, start this activity in early autumn when it is still warm and then continue to measure the temperature inside the insulated boxes over the winter months.

Ask the children if they have ever seen a bird's nest. What are they made of? Birds build nests in all sorts of places out of all sorts of materials. For example, house martins build their nests out of mud in the roofs of some buildings and warblers weave neat cups out of grass. Some even build nests on the ground or floating on water.

Birds build nests for shelter and also to lay and hatch their eggs. Baby birds growing inside eggs need to be kept warm: parent birds incubate the eggs by sitting on them, and they also find ways to insulate the nests. Some birds use hair and wool to line the insides of their nests and insulate them.

Insulation is the process of keeping heat, sound or electricity from spreading. Human houses are built with insulation (usually thick, spongy, foamy material) in the roofs and walls to try and stop heat escaping. Birds do the same with their nests, but using materials they find in their habitats.

Testing insulation

Tell the children that they are going to test out different insulation materials that birds might use, to work out which one does the best job of keeping a nest warm. The children could work in groups of two or more on their shoe box 'nests'. You can either assign a nesting material to each group or make it a competition to come up with the best combination.

Before the children start lining and filling the boxes, ask them to measure the temperature of the inside of the box with the lid on and to make a note of that and the temperature outside on that day (which can be found on weather apps etc.). They can then calculate the difference in temperature between the inside of the unlined box and the weather.

Each group of children can then line or fill their box with their natural insulation material. There is no need for them to stick the material to the inside of the box: they can simply arrange it. They can then place their thermometer inside the box and take another measurement of the temperature. Place the nests in an outdoor shed or similar and encourage the children to record the temperature of their insulated boxes once or twice a week over three months or so.

You could provide a template temperature table on handouts for the children to record the temperature showing on the thermometer inside each box, alongside the average or peak temperature of your location.

What the children will see

Encourage the children to write up their investigation and to compare the relative insulating properties of the different materials or material mixes used. Explain that the insulation in their boxes, as in bird nests, creates a barrier between the warmth of the insides of the nests and the colder outside. This reduces or slows heat transfer by decreasing thermal conduction and convection. Materials that conduct heat poorly are good thermal insulators. Materials such as feathers and hair arranged in layers are good at reducing heat loss because there are tiny air spaces where the warmth gets trapped: air is a poor conductor of heat.

Keeping nests warm using insulating materials is important for birds to ensure that eggs hatch and their chicks survive, particularly in very cold weather.

Further ideas for investigation

The children could do a linked project about how different birds build and insulate their nests and present it to the class. They could carry out another version of the experiment by building their own nests out of hay or twigs and lining these with different insulation materials.

Time for a change

Understand the difference between physical changes and chemical changes using easily found and accessible materials.

> **Links to other activities:** Another activity that covers chemical changes is 'Changing colours'. Physical changes such as melting and evaporation are covered in 'Water day', 'The heat is on' and 'Ice to see you'.

Materials

Required:

- A container, such as a jar or transparent cup
- Dry sand or fine soil and pebbles
- Ice, snow or chocolate chips

Optional:

- A twig
- Matches or a lighter (for grown-up use only)
- A garden sieve or riddle
- Bicarbonate of soda
- Lemon juice or vinegar
- Collected rainwater

Activity

This activity concentrates on how physical changes are different from chemical ones.

Mixing it up!

Ask the children, in pairs, to take a mix of sand and pebbles and put it into a container, and then to take turns to shake or swirl the container gently. What do they see happening?

Mixing is a type of physical change – and, although the sand and pebbles are mixed together, by gently shaking the container the children should see the smaller particles (the sand) go to the bottom, and the pebbles remain on top. The sand and pebbles are a mix that can be easily separated out again, by tipping out the pebbles on top. For a clearer separation, a sieve or riddle could be used.

What is a physical change?

Explain that a physical change does not result in something brand new when two or more things are brought or mixed together. You can reverse the process and get back the original 'ingredients'. Other examples of physical changes are dissolving, melting and freezing. When we mix salt or sugar in water and it dissolves, we end up with a salt or sugar solution. But if the water is evaporated off (easily done by pouring the solution onto a tray and leaving it out to dry), the solid crystals appear again.

Ask the children to hold ice, snow or chocolate chips on their hands. What happens? The warmth of their hands will melt the ice, snow or chocolate. Although it might look different, it's the same stuff: the ice or snow melts to water, but can be frozen back, and the chocolate melts but could be put in the fridge to become solid chocolate again. These are physical changes.

Further ideas for investigation

Ask the children to think about how chemical changes are different. Explain that a chemical change is where a new product is made and you can't reverse what's happened. For example, once we've baked a cake we can't get the flour back out. Examples of other chemical changes are burning, cooking, rusting, rotting and digestion. We can't get food back out of our poo!

Ask the children to try and find examples of rotting and rusting in the outdoor space. Maybe you could burn a twig as a demonstration, asking them to study the pre-burned version to see the change. What other examples can the children think of?

Give the children a teaspoon each of bicarbonate of soda, and lemon juice or vinegar, and ask them to mix them up in a container. Ask them what they see. Explain that carbon dioxide bubbles are released because a chemical reaction has happened. There is no more bicarbonate, or lemon juice or vinegar, as the reaction caused them to break up and form into new products, releasing the gas. If the children mix bicarbonate of soda with water, there won't be a reaction. Why do they think this happens? It's because this is simply dissolving the bicarbonate of soda in water, which is a physical change instead.

The big freeze

This is a simple activity for a snowy or frosty day and is a hands-on way to investigate the ice-water transition and what can affect it.

> **Links to other activities:** 'Ice to see you' is another ice-based activity that is useful to run when the weather is frosty. It also covers similar environmental themes.

Materials

Required:

- Jar lids or small dishes
- Collected rainwater
- A thermometer
- A large mixing bowl
- Salt

Optional:

- Ice cubes

Activity

Run this activity on a snowy or frosty day when the temperature is forecast to stay at freezing or below. If you know there will be a frost overnight, you could start the activity at the end of the day and then go back to it first thing the next morning.

Introduce the activity by asking the children if they have seen any ice on cars or in puddles recently. If the temperature outside is zero degrees Celsius or below, water will turn from a liquid to a solid: ice.

Tell the children that, as the weather is very cold outside, they will be able to make ice without using a freezer. Give them a jar lid each and head outside with some water in a bottle or similar. Place the jar lids in a spot where they won't be disturbed (e.g. on the ground in a corner or lined up on top of a low wall) and ask the children to pour water into each lid. The children could use a thermometer to measure the temperature of the water and the outdoors.

Return to the lids the next morning or a few hours later to see what has happened to the water. If the water has become ice, this means it has changed from a liquid to a solid. This means its particles have lost energy and don't move around: they stay in one place.

Next, the children can try to get some of the pieces of ice out of the jar lids (which a squirt of water usually shifts) and see what happens to them when they are placed in a bowl of water. Why does the ice float? Tell the children that water in its solid state is less dense than when it is liquid, which is quite unusual for substances, so ice floats on water.

Now give the children some salt to add to the pieces of ice that are still in jar lids and ask them to describe what happens. The salt will melt the ice. Explain that this is because the salt lowers the freezing point of water. It makes it harder for the water molecules to stick together.

Consider linking what the children observe in this activity to climate change by discussing the Earth's ice caps and how there are huge lumps of ice, or icebergs, floating on the sea. These are shrinking and breaking up every year due to the warming oceans.

Further ideas for investigation

On a snowy day, the children could try and clear an area of snow with salt. If you don't get many snow days, there are lots of investigations you can carry out with ice cubes outdoors. For example, you can test how long it takes for an ice cube to melt under different conditions.

1. Fill a jar or jug with cool water (e.g. from a tap or a water butt) and measure the temperature.
2. Put an ice cube into the water and time how long it takes to melt, and measure the temperature of the water again at the end.
3. Try the same thing again with water that has been warmed up by the Sun, and compare the time it takes for the ice cube to melt in the warmer water.
4. Observe the difference between melting the ice cube in the warmer water and melting it in the cooler water.

You can link this investigation to learning about glaciers and icebergs melting due to global warming. See 'Ice to see you' for a more-detailed activity on the science linking this with rising sea levels.

Changing colours

Create your own pH indicators to learn about acids, alkalis and chemical reactions.

> **Links to other activities:**
>
> - 'Time for a change' also covers chemical changes.
> - 'Paint with nature' involves natural dyes, inks and paints, which can also be used as indicators.
> - 'Rain savers' includes looking at the pH of rainwater.

Materials

Required:

- Universal pH indicator paper or litmus (for demonstration purposes)
- Bicarbonate of soda
- Vinegar
- Jar lids or small dishes

- A variety of plants that are red or purple in colour, depending on what's in season or what you can grow together, such as:
  - flowers (roses or fuchsias and their hips)
  - berries (blueberries or blackberries)
  - vegetables (red cabbage, purple cauliflower or beetroot)
- Pestles and mortars or chopping boards and jars, large stones or rolling pins
- Spoons

Optional:

- A selection of household items with varying pH levels, e.g. bananas, milk, eco washing-up liquid, lemon juice and orange juice
- Brightly coloured flowers
- Basil and mint leaves
- Aprons (to protect clothes from stains)

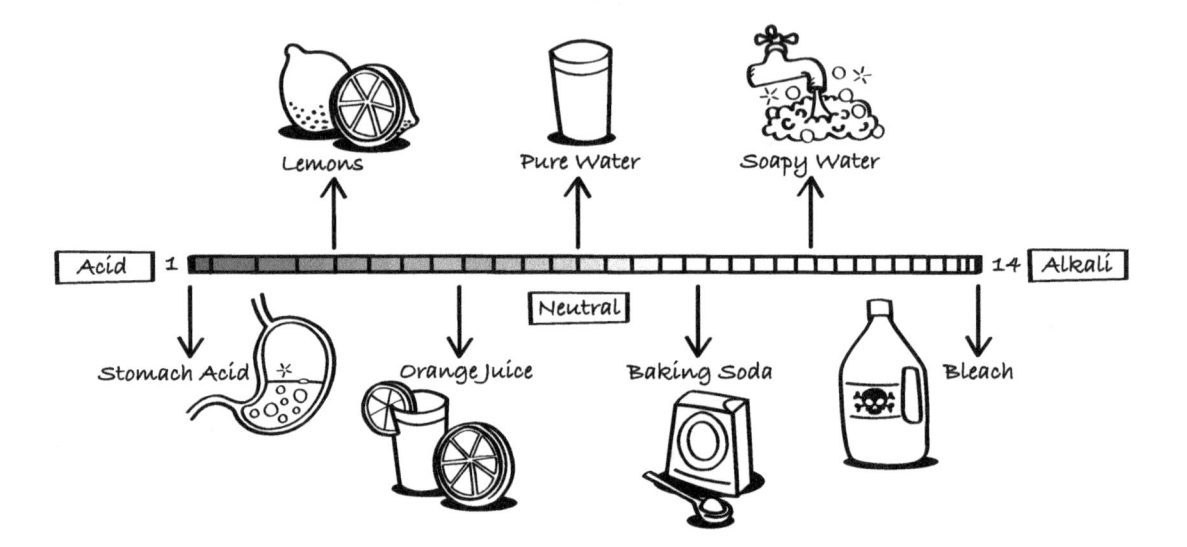

Activity

Discuss the pH scale with the class, starting off by asking them what they understand about acids. Can the children think of any examples of acids? Vinegar is one, lemon juice is another, etc. Even some fizzy sweets contain citric acid, which is what makes lemons (and other citrus fruits) sour and acidic too.

Show the children the colour-change information given with the pH paper kit and the illustration opposite. Explain that, on the pH scale, acids (vinegar and orange juice) are low in number, around 1–5 (red to orange). The other end of the scale, from 8–14 (blue to purple) is known as alkaline (or basic). We often use bicarbonate of soda, a raising agent in baking, as an example of an alkali. Soapy water is at this end of the scale too. Water is an example of a neutral liquid and is around 7 (green), in the middle of the pH scale.

The chemical reaction

Explain that, when an acid and alkali mix together, a chemical reaction happens. (This next part can be shown as a demonstration, or you can ask the children to try it themselves.) Add a pinch of bicarbonate of soda to a couple of drops of vinegar in a jar lid and see what happens. Using small amounts when demonstrating this is less costly than creating a large 'eruption' and is just as impressive. Children should notice bubbles of gas fizzing away. Explain that this is carbon dioxide gas.

Making an indicator

To find out which chemicals are acids, alkalis and neutral, we can use natural indicators instead of the more-sensitive Universal pH indicator paper. These change colour similarly to how blue litmus paper turns red in the presence of acids and red litmus turns blue in the presence of alkalis. For example, we can use the juice from blueberries to indicate what is an acid. Explain to the children that, as we know vinegar is an acid, if vinegar turns our blueberry juice (the indicator) pink, anything else that makes the blueberry juice turn pink is also an acid.

The children can set up their own investigation to observe, measure, compare and interpret their results. You can provide, or ask the children to find, red or purple berries or flowers (with guidance, as some berries may be toxic) to crush in a pestle and mortar, or on a board or on the ground by rolling a jar, large stone or rolling pin over it. Ask the children to use spoons to scoop up the juice into jar lids and to see if this juice changes colour when vinegar or bicarbonate of soda is added to it.

Red and purple flowers, fruit and vegetables (such as red roses, fuchsias, red cabbage, purple cauliflower, beetroot and blueberries) work well as indicators because they contain colour chemicals known as anthocyanins, which naturally change colour in acidic and alkaline conditions. The reddish-purple colour tends to stay the same in water, but turns a brighter pink with acids and a darker bluey-green with alkalis.

Testing the new indicator

You could give the children some other substances to test using their indicator, for example bananas, milk, eco washing-up liquid, lemon juice or orange juice. What colour does their indicator turn when added to each substance? What do the children predict and what do they conclude after testing? Could they repeat their results to check each is a real result and not a one-off finding? The children can also compare their results with others', just as scientists do in the real world.

Further ideas for investigation

The children could also try and find other coloured flowers (such as marigolds, tulips and sweet peas) or leaves and grasses and see if these can also be 'juiced' and turned into indicators. Were the children able to find other plants that worked well as indicators of acids and alkalis? If not, did these colours give them good natural dye or ink they could paint with instead?

An interesting fact to tell the children is that, in many cultures, basil and mint leaves are turned into an infusion to drink after a meal. An infusion is when the flavours of an item mix (or diffuse) into the warm water, making that water taste of it too. Infusions with leaves are known as tea.

Explain that the tea is taken after a meal because the leaves are said to help with digestion. We know that our stomachs contain acid and some people experience acid reflux or heartburn, where the stomach's acid pops up into the oesophagus making the person feel uncomfortable. As basil and mint leaves are alkaline, they have a natural neutralising effect on stomach acid, so the person feels less pain and is more relaxed. If you have any basil or mint leaves available, ask the children to crush some of those up and add a few drops of their indicator, observe the colour change and see if the leaves truly are alkaline.

The pH of the soil that we grow our plants in is really important too. Some plants such as blueberries, azaleas and rhododendrons grow in only acidic soil so are known as ericaceous (acid-loving) plants. This is to do with their root systems and the need to obtain certain nutrients from the soil, which is easier for them in acidic soils. This is why gardeners often check the pH of their soil before doing any planting.

Toppling towers

This activity involving stones, rocks or pebbles offers a fun and simple way for children to learn about gravity and forces.

> **Links to other activities:** This activity could be taught alongside 'Get over it', which also uses natural materials to learn about the various forces at play when creating structures.

Materials

Required:

- Smooth stones or rocks (ideally flat pebbles)

Optional:

- Sticks

Activity

Either ask the children to search for stones or pebbles that they think could be used to build a tower, or collect these in advance of the session for the children to use. Part of the task could be to ask the children to choose stones that would work best and create the tallest tower that doesn't topple over – in this case, you could provide a mixture of flat and smooth pebbles and more irregular-shaped rocks and stones for them to choose between. Alternatively, ask the children to find the smoothest and flattest stones from the beginning.

Challenge the children to build the tallest tower out of the pebbles or stones. Ask them to test different sizes and shapes. What do the children notice about how they need to stack the pebbles or stones? There's an element of trial and error to put each stone in such a way that it doesn't topple over, but the children should find that it's easier to start off with larger pebbles or stones and then gradually proceed to smaller ones, and where they place the smaller ones on the larger ones matters.

This is because of the stones' centre of gravity (or centre of mass). When we balance one item on top of another, there is a point at which it will stay completely equally balanced because there is an equal mass (or weight of that item) around that centre of gravity. If a stone is lopsided or an irregular shape, the centre of gravity will be closer to the heavier end of it (where there is more mass). If the centre of gravity of one stone is always directly on top of the other, the tower of stones will balance. If its centre of gravity moves slightly (i.e. when another stone is added to the top of it), the tower will collapse. Encourage the children to record the numbers of stones in their towers. Who can build the tallest tower with the highest number of stones?

Further ideas for investigation

You could introduce the word 'cairns' to the children and show photos of them from around the world. A cairn is a man-made pile of stones used as a marker. Cairns help hikers to navigate when a path is unclear. They can also have a lot of symbolic and religious meaning.

You could extend the main activity by encouraging the children to think about other natural materials that are used for building structures. You could collect sticks instead of stones and try to build towers in the style of the game Jenga®. Discuss how stacking sticks of the same length evenly creates the sturdiest tower.

Sound it out

In this activity, the children will learn about sounds and the process of hearing. Listening carefully is a vital skill and an important form of observation for scientists, especially those who work in conservation.

> **Links to other activities:** This activity acts as a good introduction to other sound- and sense-based activities such as 'Music to my ears', 'Audio trails' and 'Makes a lot of scents'. 'Bring in the bees' explains how bees' buzzing helps in pollination.

Materials

Optional:

- Speaker or device to play music
- A bird identification guide

Activity

Begin by asking the children about the five senses and then focus on hearing. What can the children hear outdoors? What is the closest sound they can hear? What is the furthest sound? They may mention birds singing, leaves rustling and wind blowing, or even cars, roadworks and aeroplanes overhead. How do they recognise these sounds?

Explain to the children that, through the process of hearing sounds, we learn to connect things to the sounds they make. We know that cats meow, dogs bark and birds sing because we've learned this. But scientists want to go a step further. For example, by knowing which birds sing particular tunes, they can identify where certain birds are nesting without actually having to see them. Birds may also use different tunes to communicate. By learning their various tunes, we can understand what they're trying to communicate, such as to warn others of danger.

Ear we go!

Ask the children to look at each other's ears. What do they look like? How far into the ear can they see? Mention that we can't see most of the ear as it's on the inside. The outside part we can see is called the pinna (or pinnae for more than one). Ask the children for examples of animals with large pinnae – perhaps rabbits and hares come to mind.

Show the children your cupped hands and place them around your ears (either both hands cupped around one ear, or each hand around each ear). Can the children do the same? Ask them if they can hear sounds better with their cupped hands or without. You could even play some music to see if the children can compare their hearing with or without cupped hands around their ears.

Pinnae are like funnels that collect up all the sound waves to direct them into our ears better. The bigger the pinnae, like when we cup our hands around our ears, the better we hear sounds.

But how do we hear sounds?

The children will understand that we communicate through sound a lot, making noises by speaking (or singing or shouting) and hearing these sounds when listening. Explain that sounds are made because something vibrates (although we don't actually see it move) and these vibrations travel through air, water and solids as sound waves. The sound waves travel through the air to our ears and make our eardrums and the little bones in our ears vibrate too. These are turned into information by the brain, which helps us understand them as sounds. Different items vibrate in different ways so we hear different sounds. Our brains make sense of it all for us.

The children may also be interested to know that being deaf or having hearing loss is when a part of the ear or the hearing system doesn't work as effectively as average, or at all. Do the children know any British Sign Language?

Further ideas for investigation

- If you're able to take the children out to a large field, ask them in pairs to stand as far away as possible from each other. When one child in the pair claps their hands, does their partner see the clap or hear it first? They should find they see the clap first. Explain that this is because sound travels much more slowly than light. This is also why we see lightning before we hear thunder.
- Ask the children to look out for different birds outdoors. Can they recognise any? You may need to use a bird identification guide to help them work out what birds they see. If they can't see any, can they hear any birdsong? Can they recognise the sounds as ones they've heard before? Crows and magpies are quite easy to identify once the children have heard them, but are there any others? The children could record sounds to identify later too.
- Ask the children to look for any bees buzzing around outside. Even the way they buzz around flowers can sound different too. The beating of bees' wings creates vibrations in the air that we hear as a buzz. The bigger the bee, the slower the wings are flapping and the lower the buzz sounds. Some bees also have a way to vibrate flowers that makes a buzzing sound. (See 'Bring in the bees' for more detail.)

Explain to the children that, while we can hear sounds, we need to learn what each sound is, which is where our brains come in. We don't suddenly hear a voice and know who it is: we learn that the voice belongs to someone, so that next time we hear it we recognise it. Our brains are amazing at remembering and pairing these memories to sounds, smells, tastes and so on. Senses actually help us learn things in such an enjoyable way that it all stays in our memories.

Spin me right 'round

Learn about friction and the physics of movement through creating natural spinning tops.

> **Links to other activities:** 'Game-changer' is another activity that looks at the physics of movement in sports and games.

Materials

Required:

- A variety of natural items such as sticks, leaves, conkers, acorns, pinecones and smooth pebbles

Optional:

- A large tray
- A conker or acorn with a nail hammered into the top
- A spinning top or coin
- Leaves (symmetrical if possible)

Activity

Ask the children if any of them have played with a spinning top. If you have one to demonstrate, show them and invite volunteers to have a go.

Take it for a spin

Ask the children to spend a few minutes outdoors looking for various items such as twigs, pebbles or conkers, and ask them to gather around a hard surface (paving, the playground or a large tray). Can the children spin the items placed on the surface? Perhaps a stick can be spun around horizontally, like a pencil. What about something heavier, or smoother? The children can take it in turns to perform their spinning to the rest of the group. Encourage the children to experiment spinning different items they've found and to think about why each does or doesn't spin. Which ones spin the longest?

You could provide the children with a conker or acorn with a nail hammered into the top or side, like a spinning top. Does it work better? What about the type of surface used for spinning on? In some tropical countries, betel nuts with a nail in the top are used as homemade spinning tops, as the slightly pointy end of the nut helps it spin.

What the children will see

Some items just won't spin that well and some items will have no trouble spinning, even if they stop after a while. Which ones did the children find worked the best? Show the children a spinning coin on a smooth surface for an example of a good spin. Could we spin a coin on grass? Twigs and the concrete ground are both quite rough, so there is a lot more friction preventing the smooth spinning. Explain that friction is the force that will stop an object sliding against a surface. The force of friction between the object and the air (also known as drag) slows the spinning down. A spinning item will only keep spinning if it can overcome the other forces.

Further ideas for investigation

Ask the children if they can think of a type of spinning actually seen in nature. Can the children find any winged seeds that spin, or a type of seed that needs the wind to carry it away (known as wind-dispersed seeds), such as on dandelion clocks? Maybe they have seen sycamore, ash or maple trees release winged seeds. Explain that the seeds of these trees are protected in coverings that have wings extending outwards. This helps them spin and fly far away from the parent tree so that they can grow in a new place without competing with their parent for nutrients in the soil. They are also less likely to be attacked by pests.

Ask the children if they can try and make their own spinners using leaves or other natural items found outdoors. The easiest idea would be to take a symmetrical leaf, cut it halfway down the middle and bend the resulting flaps in opposite directions, so they look like the blades of a helicopter. Holding the bottom part of the leaf, ask the children to throw it up in the air and watch it spin as it comes down. The type of leaf will determine the spin, so the children can experiment further.

Shadows and light

Investigate light energy and how it interacts with different objects and materials.

> **Links to other activities:** Other useful activities that cover light and plants include 'Seeds of time', 'The hole illusion', 'A-maze-ing potatoes' and 'Paint with nature'.

Materials

- A variety of leaves
- A sunny spot where objects can be held up to the light to create shadows (e.g. a wall)
- Collected rainwater (in jars)
- Large sheets of white paper
- Stones or rocks to weigh down the paper on windy days
- Mobile phones, tablets or cameras for taking photographs

Activity

Choose a sunny day for this activity. Ask the children if they have seen their shadows today. If you're already outside, ask if they can see their shadow right at that moment. What is a shadow? Explain that, when light hits an opaque (non-transparent) object, it can't go through it, so a dark area the same shape as that object appears on whatever is next to or behind it.

Shadow creatures

Tell the children they will be investigating light and shadows. In their first activity, they will create shadow creatures using leaves. First, ask them to test out creating shadows of individual leaves against a wall. They could compare the leaf shadows with their own shadows. Some leaves will create less-prominent (or you could say 'less-dark') shadows – this is because they are translucent, meaning some light from the Sun gets through. As human beings are opaque, no light will get through and their shadows will be solid.

Ask the children to try holding leaves closer to or further from the wall to investigate what happens to the sizes of the shadows. Shadows of the leaves (or any object) will 'grow' bigger the further the children hold them from the wall and get smaller when the children hold their leaves closer to the wall. This is because they are closer to the light source (the Sun) when held further from the wall, and so block out more of the light. Conversely, they block out less light when held closer to the wall because they are further from the Sun and so appear smaller.

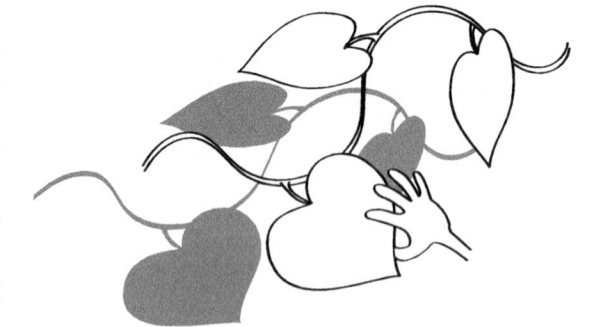

Encourage the children to try out creating different shadow shapes or creatures by holding up leaves in different arrangements. Take photos and print these out later to create a display (e.g. in the classroom).

Water, refraction and rainbows

Next, show the children the jars of water and place them onto the large sheet of paper (or use an individual piece of paper for each jar if you prefer). Move them around until a rainbow is projected by the water onto the paper. Ask the children what colours they can see in each rainbow. Explain that sunlight (and light in general) is made up of different colours and, when it hits water, these colours become visible. This is because of something called refraction. Refraction happens when light changes direction or bends when it moves from one material to another.

Light from the Sun appears to our eyes as 'white' but it is actually a mixture of the colours we see in a rainbow. Certain points are often picked out and named: violet, indigo, blue, green, yellow, orange and red. When we see a rainbow in the sky, it has been caused by sunlight passing through raindrops and splitting into these colours.

Further ideas for investigation

Demonstrate refraction by placing a paper straw or stick in the jar of water and observing how it appears to bend. You could investigate how shadows change as the Sun moves across the sky by using washable chalk. Find a wall or tree and trace the shadow of your object at different times of day, making sure to use a different colour each time and that the object doesn't move. How does the shadow change as the Sun moves across the sky?

Tendon loving care

Use materials found outdoors to demonstrate how the tendons in our bodies work.

> **Links to other activities:** 'Music to my ears' discusses ligaments in our body, which are compared to tendons here.

Materials

Required:

- A variety of leaves, preferably long, thin ones to represent fingers
- Stems such as dried grasses, lavender stalks, bean stalks or runners from bindweed or cinquefoils, or string and straightened paperclips

Optional:

- String
- Paperclips
- Smooth round rocks or pebbles
- Thin twigs

Activity

Ask the children to walk around, jump up and down, sit down and then get back up again. Have the children ever wondered how they are able to move? Ask them what their bodies are made up of in order to be able to move.

Wristy business

The children might know about the bones and the muscles inside their bodies, and how they form joints that enable us to move around freely, crawl, walk, run and jump. But have they heard of ligaments and tendons? Explain that ligaments help connect bones together, especially in joints, and tendons connect bones to muscle.

Ask the children to hold their hands out with their palms facing upwards and to look at their wrists. When they bend their fingers down to try and touch the bases of their palms, what can they see happening in their wrists? The children should see movements in their wrists because the tendons become shorter as they bend their fingers. Explain that the muscles in our arms have tendons running all the way up through our wrists into the fingers to help move the bones in our fingers.

Making a leafy finger

Ask the children to 'thread' a stem or piece of dried grass through a leaf from its stalk end to its tip, poking it in and out of the leaf in one simple running stitch. If using a sturdy stalk like lavender, bend the tip over at one end of the leaf to keep it in place. If using string, ask the children to tie a knot at the end. They can then gently pull on the other end and see what happens.

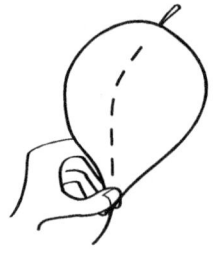

> **Teacher tip**
>
> If you can't find a suitable natural 'string' such as runners or stems and grasses, feel free to use actual string. If the natural version is not strong enough to make holes in the leaves, use a straightened paperclip to make holes in the leaves for the children.

What the children will see

The children should notice the leaf tip bending over. Explain that this is a model to help show us that tendons in our arm (the stem, grass or string in the model) run all the way up into our fingers (the leaves in the models). Pulling on a stem or string is like how the tendons shorten in our arms, to help us curl and bend our fingers, just like the leaf curls.

Further ideas for investigation

Explain the various types of joints we have in our body to the children, such as the ball-and-socket joints in our hips and the hinge joints in our elbows. Can the children use rocks, pebbles, twigs and other materials they can find outside to simulate these joints?

Guess who?

This activity will help the children understand the process of scientifically observing the natural world at close proximity by using easily available technology.

> **Links to other activities:** Other sensory activities such as 'Sound it out' and 'Makes a lot of scents' can work well together when run in a similar time period.

Materials

Required:

- A variety of natural items
- Mobile phones, tablets or cameras with zoom functions (for child use, approximately one between each group of four)

Optional:

- Leaves or plants with small hairs on them, such as borage flowers or dandelion stalks, or the leaves of tomato, potato, sage and salvia plants and hazel trees
- Hand lenses or digital microscopes

Activity

What does nature look like up close?

Split the class into groups, and ask all the children to spend a few minutes looking for a variety of natural objects to look at closely. Have one or two groups use the devices to take zoomed-in pictures of their objects, and then bring them back to the rest of the class. The next groups can then go and take their pictures. While groups are taking it in turns to do this, the rest can be using hand lenses or microscopes to study other items outdoors, or taking part in another activity or game (e.g. 'Making a splash').

Discuss with the children what observation means. Scientists need to use their eyes to look at something in really close detail, otherwise what could they miss? How do we tell the difference between two species of plants, for example? We observe the differences in flowers, leaves and seeds, and so on. Scientists need good observational skills to do their research.

What the children will see

Once all the groups have taken their pictures, show these to the whole group; they can pass around phones or cameras to see everything closely, or these can be displayed on a laptop for all to see. (If it's a sunny day, try sitting under the shade for this part and you might need to adjust the brightness settings to look at screens.) Ask the children to guess what each picture is, and then find out from the group who took it whether the guesses were correct. What do the children notice about the pictures? Was there anything surprising?

Further ideas for investigation

Other than sight, ask the children what senses they can use to find out about the specimens they chose. Scientists often use touch, sound and smell when researching wildlife. For example, there may be two roses, one smelling fragrant and the other not smelling of anything. One may have prickly thorns (so be careful) and the other not so much. Some leaves may feel soft and on closer inspection you might notice small hairs on them, such as with borage flowers, dandelion stalks and the leaves of tomato, potato, sage and salvia plants and hazel trees. If you have access to hand lenses and digital microscopes, the children might enjoy looking at other chosen specimens in even greater detail.

Seeds of time

Explore how seeds grow into plants and what different parts of the plants appear at each stage. This activity also provides opportunities to investigate what plants need to grow and spread, and how some are adapted to different climates and habitats.

> **Links to other activities:**
> - 'Bioblitz investigation' covers different plants and where they are found.
> - 'Incredible edibles', 'Seed-sational' and 'Berry nice' all cover seeds and growing plants.
> - You could also use the plants in 'Bring in the bees' and 'Sunflower power' for observations of flower visitors and pollinators. This will help the children understand how plants interact with other living things through their life cycle.

Materials

Required:

- Seeds of flowering plants (e.g. sweet peas and broad beans, which are easy to get hold of, provide good examples of plant growth and different parts of the plants)
- Glass jars
- Paper towels
- Collected rainwater
- Exercise books and pencils (for plant journals)

Optional:

- Small recycled plastic or homemade plant pots (as in 'Making recycled plant pots' on page 45)
- Peat-free compost
- Mobile phones, tablets or cameras for taking time-lapse photographs

Activity

Invite the children to look at the seeds and describe how they look and feel. What is inside each seed? How does a seed grow into a plant? Ask the children to think about what it might need to germinate. (This is a good opportunity to introduce this word and explain that it means 'to start growing'.) Discuss how soaking the seeds in water might be a good way to start germination and talk about what is inside a seed: they contain starch, which is stored energy to allow the baby plants to start to grow.

Put the seeds in a jar of water overnight or over a weekend. Afterwards, get them out of the water and give each group of children (groups of up to four) two to four seeds and one piece of paper towel. Ask the children to dampen their paper towel and then lay it out flat and place their seeds onto it, keeping them on one half of the towel.

Ask the children to fold each paper towel back on itself and carefully place each paper towel into a jar, with the seeds pointing 'outwards' and visible. Some seeds might fall off or move around but the children can reach into their jars and move them back to where they were.

Put the jars in a sunny spot. (If you don't have a large enough outside space, or it's a cold time of year, take them into the classroom and put them on or near a window ledge.) You could also place some of the jars in darker, shaded spots to compare growth under different conditions.

Encourage the children to record what they observe in their jars on a daily basis. Bean seeds, for example, will start to germinate within 24 hours if you've soaked them. Depending on their age, the children could draw labelled diagrams or similar. The first step to record is the seed coat breaking open followed by the emergence of the root to find water and then the shoot to find light. This is followed by the appearance of the first leaves (or cotyledons).

Tracking growth

After two weeks, transfer the seedlings into pots of compost or soil. (See 'Making recycled plant pots' below.)

Activity

Making recycled plant pots

Materials:

- Cardboard or newspaper
- Scissors
- Water
- Jars or tins (ideally a variety of cylindrical objects for making a range of different pot sizes)
- Peat-free compost
- Seeds

Method:

1. Remove any labels or tape from the cardboard. (You can also use layers of wet newspaper to make these handy pots.) Soak the cardboard in water for 30 minutes.
2. Cut the soaked cardboard into strips.
3. Wrap the strips around the sides and bottom of each cylindrical object.
4. Leave them to dry in a sunny spot. Make sure you remove the cardboard shell from the object before the cardboard dries completely or it'll stick fast.
5. Fill your pots with your compost mix and plant your seeds. (If your seedlings are going to be planted on into flower beds you can plant the whole pot, as the cardboard will decompose in the soil.)

Encourage the children to continue recording their plant's development (perhaps on a weekly basis or every time they water them once they are transferred to soil). When more leaves appear, you can talk about what 'job' they do for the plant, i.e. they use the Sun's energy and carbon dioxide from the air to make sugars for the plant so it can grow.

Continue to track the growth and development of the plants until they have produced flowers, fruits (or pods) and seeds. The children can then draw full life cycles of their plants. Talk about what plants need to go through all stages of their life cycles: light, water, oxygen, carbon dioxide and their ideal temperature.

One option is to take a photo each day using a smartphone or camera and to use these to create a timeline of growth. If possible, you could print these out to make an engaging physical display that 'grows' around the classroom walls over time. If you're very tech-savvy, you could set up a camera that films one of the plants for the whole time, and then create a time-lapse video of the seed germinating and growing the first parts of the young plant.

Further ideas for investigation

Ask the children to record whether each sprouting seed is growing in a clockwise or anticlockwise direction. This will always be the same for a particular plant. (For example, beans always grow in an anticlockwise spiral, whereas honeysuckle grows in a clockwise direction.) This is dependent on the type of plant and their genes.

You could record the growth of different types of plants to compare them, perhaps with photos of the different stages set out in a timeline as outlined above. This would be a very visual way of discussing different types of flowers, fruits, seeds and dispersal.

The children could investigate how different types of plant are 'adapted' to different environments. For example, seaweed likes to grow in very salty, wet conditions and cacti grow well in hot, dry environments.

Sunflower power

Sunflowers offer a world of discovery for children as we can grow them easily from seed. In this activity, sunflower plants are used throughout their life cycle, leading to simple maths games and learning about seed production and food chains.

> **Links to other activities:** Other growing-based activities include 'Seeds of time', 'Seed-sational', 'Berry nice' and 'Can weeds help us?'.

Materials

Required:

- Sunflower plants, grown in small recycled plastic or homemade plant pots (as in 'Making recycled plant pots' on page 45)
- Paper bags
- String
- Exercise books and pencils (for plant journals and to keep tally in the counting activity)
- Trays

Optional:

- A packet of sunflower seeds for growing from seed or demonstration purposes only (ideally dwarf varieties, which are perfect for growing in smaller spaces)
- Peat-free compost
- Bird identification guides
- Wooden lolly sticks (for labelling plants)
- Mobile phones, tablets or cameras for taking time-lapse photographs

Activity

Sow your seeds

An optional first step is to make pots out of recycled cardboard or newspaper (as in 'Making recycled plant pots' on page 45). Alternatively, ask each child to bring in a recycled pot (such as a large yoghurt pot) to use as a planter. (Drainage holes will need to be made in the bottom of any reused plastic containers – adults can do this using a screwdriver or similar.) Ask each of them to plant a sunflower seed in some compost in their pot. Each child can label their sunflower with their name on a lolly stick or similar.

Alternatively, sow some sunflower seeds yourself in advance: either in pots so there are enough for one per child in the group or, if you have a bare flower-bed, you can sow the seeds directly into the ground. (The best time for planting is late April or May, to carry out the harvesting in September or October.) This activity is best carried out on a bright, sunny day.

Enjoying and harvesting the sunflowers

Encourage the children to make weekly observations of their sunflowers so they can discuss and enjoy each stage from seedling to flowering. Run weekly 'sunflower safaris' where the children investigate what insects and other animals are living or feeding on their sunflowers. Create a timeline of different species that are found on the sunflowers, from when the plants are seedlings to when they are dried out and full of seeds.

When you notice that the sunflowers are drooping, their petals are falling away and the backs of them are turning brown, this is the start of them going to seed and drying out. When this happens, place a large paper bag over the top of each flower-head and tie it with string. This helps the flower-head to dry out, prevents (or at least reduces) predation of the seeds and catches any seeds that become loose.

After two to four weeks, collect in the sunflower flower-heads (which may well have become very droopy by this point) and split them into two groups. One half of them will be used for a seed-counting maths challenge and the other will be used to create natural bird feeders.

Seed-counting challenge

For the counting challenge, ask the children to count the seeds of each of the dried-out flower-heads in turn. To do this they can use a tray to empty out any loose seeds from the paper bag and then can pinch out the rest onto the tray. Depending on the number of trays you have, you could encourage the children to work in pairs or small groups with one flower-head per group so they can work together to count the seeds. One child could keep a tally as another child counts out loud. Ask them to work together as a whole group to work out the total number of seeds in all the sunflowers they've counted, and then to work out the average number of seeds per sunflower. Use the leftover seeds to feed birds on a bird table or similar, to create natural bird feeders (as in 'Making natural bird-feeders' below) or store them in envelopes to sow next year.

> **Teacher tip**
>
> Depending on the variety of sunflower, there are usually around one thousand seeds in a sunflower head (and some have up to two thousand) – so counting might take a while. For younger groups, you can simply ask them to use the seeds to count up to 10 or 100, or do some basic arithmetic.

Making natural bird feeders

Materials:

- A screwdriver (for grown-up use only)
- Wire

Method:

For the natural bird-feeder activity, make two holes on opposite sides of the sunflower heads using a screwdriver (at nine o'clock and three o'clock). Then help the children to thread wire or string through the holes and hang their flower-head bird feeders on fences or in trees. Try to space them out around the site.

Birdwatching

Create a birdwatching rota and ask the children to record bird feeding visits on one or more of the feeders. (See 'Making natural bird feeders' above.) You could give them simple bird identification guides so they can make a note of which common species eat the seeds. (See 'Making natural bird-feeders' above.) When all the seeds have been eaten, collect in the sunflower heads and put them on a compost heap or in green waste for council collection.

The children could look at all the bird visits recorded while the sunflower heads were hanging up and discuss what types of bird made the most visits to eat seeds. Hopefully, the children will have seen a few different species of bird. Sunflower seeds are most popular with blackbirds, blue tits, goldfinches, greenfinches and woodpeckers. Talk to the children about why birds like to eat sunflower seeds: they are packed with minerals such as potassium, calcium, magnesium, vitamin B6 and iron. They are also high in protein, fibre and polyunsaturated fat. These nutrients keep birds healthy through the winter months.

Discuss the role of a sunflower in a food chain. How did the sunflower make food to grow? What kinds of pollinators visited the sunflower while it was blooming? Which animals will eat the seeds it produced? What will happen to the rest of the plant now it has died? Link this discussion to your lessons about food chains, decomposition and biodiversity.

Linking the activities

You could also link the maths activity with the bird-feeder activity by asking the children to estimate the total number of seeds produced from all of the sunflowers grown. (Older children can think about the calculation they need to do in order to work this out.) Then discuss how many of those seeds might end up as new sunflowers and how many might be eaten by birds or other animals if they were left to grow in the wild.

Further ideas for investigation

On a sunny day, set up a camera so it points at a young sunflower and create a time-lapse film of the sunflower moving with the Sun over the course of a day. The reason young sunflowers move with the Sun (i.e. face east in the morning and west in the evening) is so they can receive the most light for photosynthesis. This won't happen in older sunflowers as they stay facing east. This is because facing east warms their flowers up and attracts more bees for pollination.

Sum it up

Mathematics is important in our daily lives, but even more so in science. In this activity, the children will use leaves to learn about measuring and counting, which is perfect for young learners. The children will already know how to use rulers for measuring, but what if what they're trying to measure is not straight?

> **Links to other activities:** 'Can weeds help us?', 'Sunflower power' and 'Bioblitz investigation' all include some maths-based activities, and 'What was here before us?' also covers how to find out the ages of trees.

Materials

Required:

- A variety of leaves (ideally oak and horse chestnut leaves, which are particularly fun for this activity)
- String or wool
- Metre rulers

Optional:

- Calculators
- Marker pens
- Scissors

Activity

Stringing along

Find out if the children remember or know what the perimeter of an object is. Explain that it is the distance all the way around the outside of the object, such as a leaf. See if the children can work out a way to measure the perimeter using a metre ruler. Can they? Ask them why it would be difficult. The leaves definitely don't have straight edges.

Show the children how they can use a piece of string starting at one end of the leaf (closest to the stalk) and taking it around the whole leaf, as if tracing it with the string (as in the illustration) to find out the perimeter. The children can follow along with their string and leaves. If they find it difficult to hold onto the string, they can use a marker pen to mark how far long the leaf and string they measured up to.

Ask them to take the piece of string (marked by holding with their finger and thumb or a marker pen, or cut to size with scissors) and measure it against the metre ruler. Find out whose leaf had the longest perimeter. Were the children surprised by the findings? Take photos of the children holding their pieces of string and their leaves for a school display.

More mathematical fun outdoors

Where else can the children use maths outdoors? Can the children spot any geometry outdoors? What shapes can they see? Perhaps they wish to count the number of flowers on a particular plant, or the number of woodlice in a shaded area. How would they go about estimating the number of all the woodlice in a huge shaded area, just by knowing how many are in a small area? Some children may have already taken part in community Bioblitzes (as in the 'Bioblitz investigation', page 57), garden bird counts and other citizen science activities without thinking of them as science, maths or research.

Further ideas for investigation

Ask the children if they've ever learned how to tell the age of a tree. Some might say that you take a slice of the trunk and then count the rings to work out how old the tree is. But what if you don't want to cut the tree down?

Explain to the children that there is a lovely mathematical way we can estimate, or get an idea, of how old a tree is. Ask the children to find their favourite tree that they'd like to know the age of. Then they need to measure its girth, which is the circumference of the trunk. Using the metre ruler, ask them to find where the tree is one metre high from the ground. Then ask the children to use a piece of string to measure around the trunk of the tree at this point. They can then use the string against the metre ruler to find out the tree's girth in centimetres.

The children can then divide this measurement by 2.5 cm, as this is how much trees typically grow per year, on average. As the precise rate of growth is different depending on the tree, different numbers may be used. For example, oak trees grow slowly so the girth measurement can be divided by 1.88 cm and pine trees grow quickly so it can be divided by 3.13 cm. The children can use calculators to be accurate, but could alternatively simply halve their tree-girth measurement to work out an approximate age. Find out what they think about this method and their results.

A-maze-ing potatoes

Learn how to grow food, such as potatoes, to understand food security and food waste better.

> **Links to other activities:** 'Berry nice', 'Bring in the bees' and 'Incredible edibles' also cover food that can be grown and eaten.

Materials

Required:

- A small potato or seed potato
- A small cardboard box such as a shoe box, or a dark enclosed space outdoors (e.g. an empty bin or a bucket with a lid)
- Recycled paper tape
- Scissors

Optional:

- Pieces of card or cardboard
- A large pot of soil or peat-free compost

Activity

Ask the children when they last ate potatoes and how these were cooked. Did they enjoy their meal? Do any of them know how and where potatoes grow? Explain to the children that a potato is an edible stem tuber, the energy storage part of a plant, and that potatoes are from the same plant family as tomatoes. They give us lots of energy as they are high in starch, which is a carbohydrate. Eating the skins is good for us too, as they are full of fibre.

How potatoes grow

Ask the children if they've ever seen 'eyes' on potatoes. This occurs because potatoes tend to sprout (or chit), which means they're getting ready for planting. This activity shows how potato plants find the light, and can be done in groups or as a class.

Help the children cut a hole roughly 2 cm in diameter in the short side of a cardboard box, such as a shoebox (with a lid). To make it really maze-like, use pieces of card with slightly different widths or heights and help the children tape these inside the box as maze dividers (as in the illustration below). Explain to the children that the gaps will let light travel through the main hole into the box from the outside.

Ask the children to place the sprouting potato into the side of the box without the hole in it, close the lid and leave it somewhere where the hole in the box points towards a sunny window. What do the children think the potato sprouts will do?

> **Teacher tip**
>
> If the cardboard maze is too complicated, the children can place the potatoes in an empty bucket somewhere dark, with a lid slightly tilted so that a little bit of light can get through.

What the children will see

In a few days, you can open the lid and see what's happened. The children should notice that the sprouted parts of the potato (the shoots) are growing towards the light. What happens if they leave the potatoes even longer? The children should see the sprouts make their way through the maze.

Explain that all plants, including potatoes, have light-sensitive cells that make them grow towards the light, and this is why the sprouts bend in that direction. Chlorophyll, the green pigment needed for photosynthesis, can't be formed in the dark, so the shoots are yellow-white in colour. Potatoes can sit underground for a while and, when the conditions are right, they start sprouting towards the light. This means that huge leaves can grow above ground, feeding more potatoes underground. Small or seed potatoes can be re-planted to give us many more potatoes.

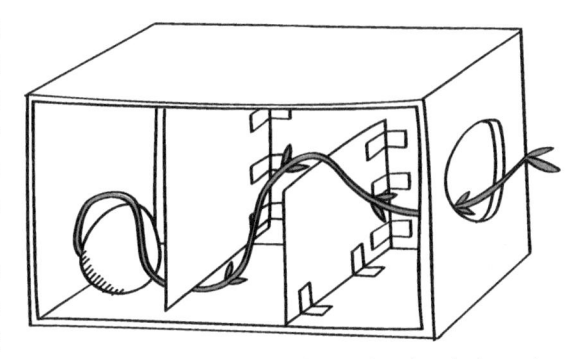

Further ideas for investigation

Normally, the potatoes can be planted once the sprouts are about 2 cm long. The children could take this activity further by taking the sprouted potatoes and planting them into the ground, or into a large pot of compost kept somewhere sunny. The children can water them whenever the compost is dry. Ask the children to record when the leaves appear. At this point, the plants can be covered completely with soil or compost. Explain that this is known as 'earthing up' and is important to stop light getting to the developing potatoes. Light makes potatoes go green, and green potatoes are poisonous because of an increase in a toxin called solanine.

You're the lichen to my moss

Learn about moss in your lawn and lichen on your fence, and find out what they tell us about our local environment and how they can help us navigate its changes.

> **Links to other activities:** This can be used within the identification and classification activity 'Bioblitz investigation'. The terrarium activity in 'Further ideas for investigation' also links to the water cycle and evaporation, as in 'Water Day'.

Materials

Required:

- Hand lenses
- Exercise books and pencils (to fill in the lichen and moss chart)

Optional:

- A moss and lichen identification guide

Activity

Ask the children if they know what a moss is – a plant or something else. Explain it is a type of plant but a very ancient one (which was around before the dinosaurs) that doesn't have flowers or seeds. Most mosses do need sunshine and water to grow, like flowering plants, but they reproduce in a different way.

Lots of mosses like to grow in damp places. Ask the children if they have seen any moss growing in the school playground or local area. You might find mosses growing on the trunks of trees and shrubs, hard surfaces, borders and the top of compost in containers. Mosses have cousins called liverworts and hornworts, which are also small plants and have the same life cycles as mosses.

Have the children heard of lichens? Tell them that these grow in similar places to moss but that they are very different: lichens are actually two living things working together to grow. Explain that a lichen is both fungus (a living thing that is not a plant or animal) and a tiny living thing called algae (a very simple plant) growing together. Both of these different living parts of a lichen get something out of growing together. The fungus part gets sugars made by the algae, which carries out photosynthesis, and the algae gets protection and help from the fungus to absorb water. You might spot lichens growing on wooden fences, trees or rocks.

Lichen or moss?

Take the children out to the school playground or a local green space and ask them to go on a moss and lichen hunt. If you can, give them each a hand lens and an exercise book, and encourage them to record each lichen and moss they find. Use the following table:

What is it? A lichen or a moss?	
Where is it growing? Describe the place you found it and what the conditions are (e.g. damp, dry, light or shady).	
What does it look like? Describe the colour, size, shape, etc.	
What does it feel like? Is it soft or hard?	
Draw a picture of your lichen or moss. You could draw what it looks like, where it is growing and also what you see when you look under the hand lens.	

There are some good introductory guides to lichens and mosses available. (The Field Studies Council has some great, inexpensive nature guides on their website.) Borrowing one from your local library or buying a couple of copies can be a great way for the children to try and work out the names of the different mosses and lichens they find.

Thinking about habitats

Encourage the children to carry on their lichen and moss hunting and recording when they're at home, out in parks, etc. Tell them that lichens are a good indicator of air pollution – some types of lichen will grow only where the air is low in pollutants such as petrol and diesel engine fumes. The children could find out from books or online what types of lichen to look out for and carry out a local survey of lichens to investigate where air pollution is higher and lower.

Using the hand lenses to investigate the amazing structures of mosses and lichens is a great way for children to understand how different types of living things are adapted to the habitats where they live, and how they support other living things. For example, the children can use hand lenses to look at moss 'leaflets', which absorb water. You can talk about how mosses act like sponges and suck up rainwater, helping to keep the habitats they grow in damp, and other plants to grow. The children can also look at the hair-like structures (called rhizoids) that anchor mosses to whatever they're growing on. Talk about how these are different from the more-branched roots they might have seen on bigger plants.

You can use small amounts of moss to make mini moss terrariums as a way of observing how moss absorbs water. This activity is best carried out in groups so that the children only collect a small amount of moss from a particular site.

Further ideas for investigation

Making a mini moss terrarium

Materials:

Required:

- A jam jar or wide-necked glass bottle
- A mix of gravel, stones and soil
- Moss
- Water
- A mister or spray bottle

Optional:

- Activated charcoal
- Decorative natural items, such as pebbles, acorns or tree roots
- Recycled paper tape

Method:

1. Add a mix of gravel, stones and soil to your jam jar or glass bottle – about 2.5 cm in depth is fine. (You might consider adding activated charcoal in the bottom of the jar, as this stops bacteria growing and helps the terrarium last a bit longer – you can get this quite cheaply in pet shops and online.)
2. Add a small amount of moss collected from your local area to this, and then some water.
3. The children can get creative with adding some decorative scenery to their mini moss habitats, such as pretty pebbles, acorns or pieces of tree root.
4. Give the terrarium a spray of water with a mister or spray bottle when it's complete. If you can, seal it with tape and keep it somewhere light and warm (but not too hot). Further watering shouldn't be required as terrariums can usually maintain their own mini water cycles.

You can link this activity with 'Water day', which includes observations of evaporation – terrariums are a great visual way to stimulate discussions about evaporation, condensation and transpiration.

Bioblitz investigation

Get the children excited about biodiversity and wildlife by running your own Bioblitz. Getting hands-on with minibeasts and other wildlife can help support learning around habitats, adaptation and ecosystems.

> **Links to other activities:** As this activity is all about biodiversity, you might like to have a look at the following activities too, which cover a variety of plant and animal species:
>
> - Seeds of time
> - You're the lichen to my moss
> - What on earth?
> - The wonderful world of worms
> - Bring in the bees.

Materials

Required:

- Tables
- Trays with sides so crawling minibeasts can't easily escape (ideally white)
- Glass jars (with lids and labels removed)
- Exercise books and pencils
- Hand lenses
- Discs of paper or cloth to be used as breathable lids on the jars (with tiny air holes made using a needle or pin before the activity session – only needed for insects that are likely to fly away)
- Wildlife identification guides or books (some of which are available free from online primary teaching sites; alternatively, check the Field Studies Council website for advice on the best guides for the age group you're working with)
- Insect bite cream and antihistamines

Optional:

- Scissors, tweezers or both
- Flipchart or whiteboard and pens
- Mobile phone, tablet or camera for taking photographs
- Non-thorny plant samples (e.g. bean, pea, strawberry, daffodil, sunflower, dandelion and nasturtium plants) that include flowers, buds, leaves, stems, seeds, fruits, seed-pods and roots
- Large sheets of reused paper or card
- Hand lenses

Safety note

We recommend having an EpiPen® on site with a First Aider who is trained in using it for this activity. Even if none of the children or adults has known allergies to bee or wasp stings, severe allergic reactions can occur suddenly without any previous episodes.

Activity

Fact file: Bioblitzes

A Bioblitz is a timed activity where you record all living things in a specific location (e.g. a park). You can find lots of living things even in a short Bioblitz, especially if you have lots of keen children doing the searching.

You can limit your Bioblitz to just an hour, or make a longer event out of it (even a whole day) and invite parents/carers. If you decide to make it an event, why not contact your local wildlife trust or natural history society? Ask if they can help by sending a volunteer or two who can help with searching for and identifying minibeasts, plants and fungi and so on. They can also help link you up with a citizen science initiative, giving the chance for the children to get involved in real science data collection.

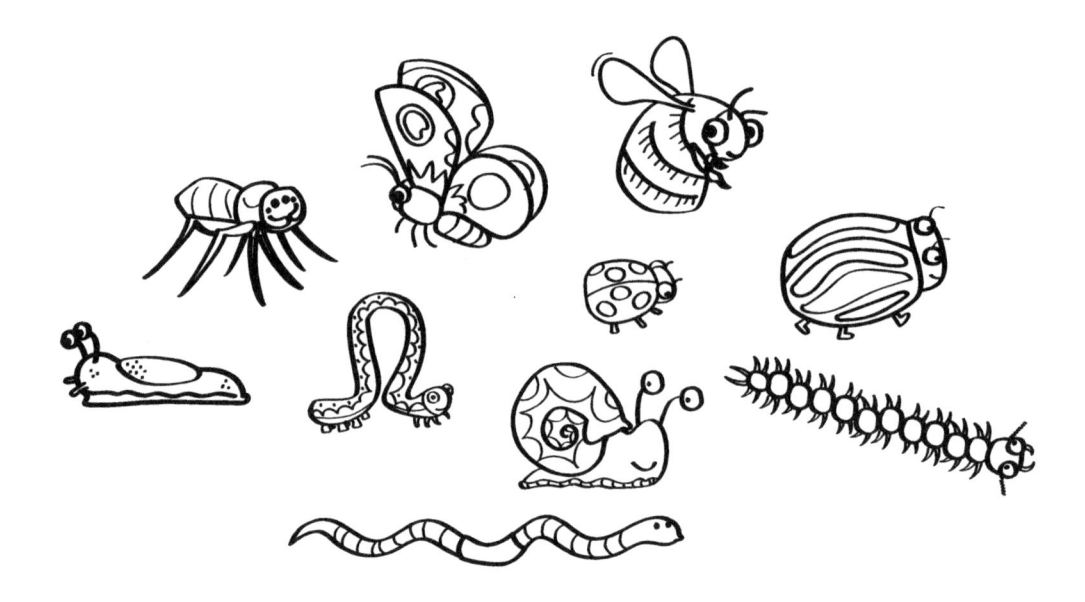

Collecting minibeasts

Set up a 'base' for the Bioblitz – put out a few tables and lay out the trays and wildlife identification guides (if using). Tell the children they will each be given a jar, an exercise book and a pencil. Challenge the children to find as many living things as they can in a particular area (e.g. the school playground, a field or a local park) and collect them in their jars. Minibeasts (or invertebrates) that live in soil or underground, such as beetles, worms and snails, are some of the easiest types of wildlife to collect. Encourage the children to search for minibeasts in damp corners, under logs and leaves, on tree trunks and in plant foliage (e.g. for aphids and ladybirds).

Ask the children to bring the minibeasts that they collect in their pots or jars to the base table and tip them into the trays. Encourage them to look through identification guides or wildlife books to try and work out which species or families of invertebrates they belong to and to write them down. The children could keep a tally of how many individual minibeasts they collect, and they could also contribute to a list of species (e.g. on a central whiteboard or flipchart next to the tables) so there is a visual record of how many different species have been collected as the session progresses.

> **Teacher tip**
>
> At the end of the session, ensure all minibeasts are returned to the area of the Bioblitz site they were collected from. Plants and fungi can be recorded (e.g. with a mobile phone), but these should ideally be left where they're growing and not picked or collected.

Collecting winged insects

For winged insects such as bees, wasps and butterflies, some can safely be collected by adults. For example, a bumblebee on a flower can be coaxed into a jar with a paper or cloth lid with air holes punched in them for a short amount of time. Once the children have had a look at a bee in the jar, and you've recorded what species you think it is, let the bee fly off or it could get distressed. It is best to avoid trying to catch butterflies as they are easily damaged. Instead, you could take a photo on a mobile phone and the children can use that to identify the species and record it.

Remind the children to not collect bees or hoverflies themselves but to ask an adult to help, to avoid risk of stings and allergic reactions. Adults should not try to collect bees if they have a known allergy to bee stings. Keep bite cream and antihistamines on hand in case of stings and allergic reactions.

Species and habitats

You can use a Bioblitz to lead into discussions about habitats and why different types of wildlife are found in different places. You can use the example of insects as a group to discuss what we mean by 'species'. For example, all insects share some common features, like having six legs, but there are lots of different species amongst this group and they have differently shaped and coloured bodies, and they eat different foods.

Different species of insects are adapted to different habitats. For example, butterflies are adapted to life in the air, and have wings and long tongues allowing them to fly from flower to flower and suck up the sugary nectar. By comparison, beetles are dark coloured and have special mouthparts so they can thrive in damp areas of soil where they can hide from predators, and use their strong jaws to feed on tough plant matter.

Further ideas for investigation

Challenge the children to find as many different habitats as they can in an outdoor space. Encourage them to lift up old logs or large stones (where hopefully they'll find some beetles, centipedes and other damp-loving minibeasts) and to look on fences and in pavement cracks (for weeds, lichens and mosses). They can then record what living things they find in each habitat. This can lead to discussions about how different species are adapted for different habitats. A follow-up investigation could involve the children trying to create habitats, such as by placing old cardboard down in a shady place or piling up logs and leaf material, and seeing what wildlife lives there over time. They could also simply clear an area of soil and see what plants grow there first.

Introduce the idea of classification of wildlife, and adaptation, by dissecting different types of plants and comparing them. Collect a range of non-thorny plant samples (e.g. bean, pea, strawberry, daffodil, sunflower, dandelion and nasturtium plants). If possible, each sample should include some or all of these resources: flowers, buds, leaves, stems, seeds, fruits, seed-pods and roots. Encourage the children to use tweezers and safety scissors to dissect out the different parts of each type of plant and lay them out on large sheets of reused paper or card. Challenge them to try and label the different parts and discuss how different the seeds, flowers, leaves etc. are in different plant species and families. They can use magnifying glasses or hand lenses to get a closer look. If you have any scientific diagrams of the parts of a flower, you could use this to show how important it is to look at real-life examples of a range of plant species to find out how they actually look – very few of them will resemble the 'typical' flower shown in scientific diagrams.

Section 2

Science games

Game-changer

This activity enables the children to understand how important the laws of physics have been when inventing various sports. Can the children devise their own games using what they understand about physics?

> **Links to other activities:** The following activities contain a game element as well as learning about the physics of movement, so you might like to run them together over a period of time under a science games theme:
>
> - Leaf me to race
> - Spin me right 'round
> - Making a splash
> - Poohsticks.

Materials

Required:

- A shuttlecock
- A variety of natural items such as feathers, leaves, acorns, conkers, pinecones, twigs, branches and grasses

Optional:

- String
- Small lightweight tennis ball and bat (for demonstration purposes)

Activity

Explain to the children that tennis was invented many years ago, and back then a ball was hit using the palm of the hand (later with gloves on), instead of a racket. The balls were made of rubber, or an outer covering of leather or cloth filled with scraps of material or horsehair. The first badminton shuttlecock was made with cork and feathers. Cricket bats were (and still are) made using wood from willow trees.

Ask the children what they think about sports and games that use natural materials. What kinds of material do they see in sports these days? You could ask them if they knew that rugby balls were originally made from pig bladders, which is why they have a more-oval shape.

The shuttlecock

Show the children a modern shuttlecock, and explain that they're usually made of plastic these days. Can the children make their own shuttlecocks using items they've found outdoors? Strong grasses, stems or string could be used to tie leaves or feathers to pieces of twig, flower buds, rosehips or acorns. The children can try throwing them up in the air and tapping them with their palms or a bat to see how they fly and fall. Do they stay intact?

Inventing a natural sports game

The children can work in pairs or small groups either to come up with brand-new sports games or to turn a current game into a more environmentally friendly, natural one. What are the rules if it's a new game, and how will they create the various components or equipment out of what's available in the outdoor environment? Discuss with the children the elements of the games: will there be rackets or bats, and a type of ball? How will players score, maybe using goal posts, nets or baskets? How does being outdoors affect their games? The weather, especially the wind, can have an effect on how a ball flies through the air or between posts. Can the children run quickly against the wind?

> **Safety note**
>
> Make sure no children plan to throw around stones or pebbles at each other in their new games. If you are concerned about objects flying into children, why not stick to feathers to create a 'ball' game?

What the children will see

Thinking about their games and the materials used, what do the children think of the way their games worked? How did they hit the 'balls' or 'shuttlecocks'? How did these travel through the air?

Explain that, as an item flies through the air, it has the forces of gravity pulling it down and air resistance (friction between the object and air, also known as drag) trying to stop it continuing. To keep it in the air we have to hit it, generating a force of lift. Shuttlecocks were made with feathers and cork to slow them down further, so they don't fall to the ground as quickly as a heavier ball. The most streamlined, aerodynamic shape is a teardrop, as its smooth shape reduces drag. What do the children think of this in terms of the shape of a traditional shuttlecock?

Further ideas for investigation

The children might also want to think about how to put a spin on a ball flying through the air, such as in cricket spin-bowling. This is when the bowler uses their wrist or finger to give a spin to the ball when they throw it. This causes the ball to spin so much that it can drift sideways in the air before or after the bounce, making it difficult for the batter to hit it, and is known as the Magnus effect. This effect is also seen when a footballer 'bends' or 'curves' a ball, like during a free kick.

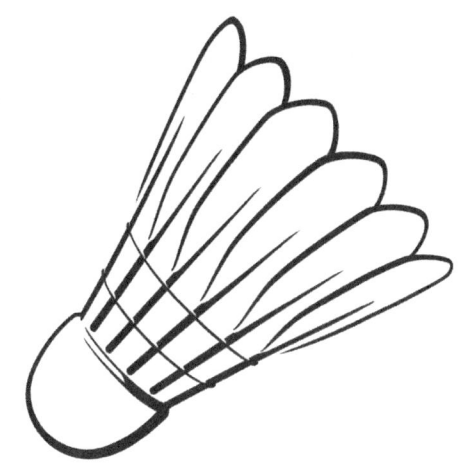

Making a splash

This activity encourages the children to learn about the properties of water through playing a game that harnesses the power of surface tension.

> **Links to other activities:** 'Leaf me to race' discusses the property of surface tension, while 'Toppling towers' and 'Game-changer' are other game-based activities exploring forces and movement.

Materials

Required:

- Jar lids or small dishes
- Collected rainwater
- Bottle lids, acorn caps or similar small containers

Optional:

- A leaf or feather

Activity

Ask the children what they think a raindrop looks like. They might describe a teardrop or other streamlined shape. Explain that small rain droplets are actually only perfectly spherical for a short time. As they fall down through the sky (through the air molecules), they squish into a shape resembling a burger bun. If the droplets are big enough, we see them split into teardrop shapes. (We tend to think raindrops are always teardrop-shaped because of how water droplets look when they drip from our taps.)

Section 2: Science games

If the children would like to see a droplet, ask each to dip a finger into a small container of water and place a droplet onto a leaf or feather. What can they see? Explain that, as water molecules are like tiny magnets, they all pull towards each other and form a sphere, like a ball.

What is surface tension?

Surface tension is the ability of water molecules to pull towards each other, and form an invisible 'skin' on the surface. It's is useful for creatures such as pond skaters to glide across a pond searching for prey. (For a more detailed explanation, see 'Leaf me to race'.)

Explain that this is also useful for a game. Ask the children, either as a whole class or in groups, to take turns to pour a small amount of rainwater from a bottle lid or acorn cup into a jar lid or jar. The water will slowly start to fill up the lid or jar. Explain that the person who makes water spill over the edges loses (or has to fulfil a task, such as cleaning up after the activity). If you like, the winner is the last person to pour water in successfully before the spillage.

What the children will see

As each child pours water in, even though the water level reaches the top of the lid or jar, there is still 'space' somehow for more water to be added. Explain to the children that this is because of the surface tension of water. The water molecules are attracted to each other, meaning they make as much space as possible for all the molecules until there are too many and some water has to escape.

Further ideas for investigation

The children can add droplets one by one to a leaf or feather, and then see what happens if they add droplets very close to each other. What happens when droplets meet? Explain that the water molecules all come together to create a larger droplet, as the easiest shape to form is a sphere – a bit like bubbles.

The children should find that water droplets roll straight off feathers because of the oils on the surface. Can the children create such water spheres on their clothes, or do they get absorbed by the material?

Poohsticks

This is the perfect science link for World Book Day, Winnie the Pooh Day, National Storytelling Week, Book Week or to kick off a summer reading challenge. The children will have the chance to play their favourite bear's favourite game while learning about water resistance, density and streamlining.

Links to other activities: The following activities have great links for learning about the properties of water:

- 'Game-changer' and 'Spin me right 'round' cover streamlining, friction and the physics of movement.
- 'That sinking feeling' is all about floating and sinking.
- 'Leaf me to race' and 'Making a splash' use water's surface tension to create fun race games.

Materials

Required:

- Access to a stream or similar with a bridge over it (or a pond, a fountain or even a puddle)
- A variety of sticks and twigs of varying shapes and sizes, ensuring that:
  - enough sticks and twigs are collected that the children can choose up to three different ones
  - some are very straight and thin, others are thick and some have short side branches
  - if using a puddle, very small sticks or even pine needles
- A stopwatch

Optional:

- A variety of natural items that float, e.g. leaves, flowers, feathers, pinecones and seed heads

Activity

Depending on the age group of the children, you could start this activity by reading *Pooh Invents a New Game* by A. A. Milne, perhaps during Book Week. Tell the children they are going to play Poohsticks. Show them the collection of sticks and twigs and ask them each to choose three sticks (and one other object if you have these) for the Poohsticks races. Ask them what shape and size of stick they think will be the fastest at moving through flowing water.

At the water, ask the children to use their first sticks to test out what direction the race will go in: this will give them the chance to observe and discuss the direction of flow in the stream or pond. In a stream, the flow will be going downhill due to gravity; in a pond, the wind direction will affect the movement of objects in the water. If there is very little wind or you're using a puddle, you can perhaps choose very small sticks or pine needles and create wind by blowing on them.

The children can then choose their sticks for the first Poohsticks race. Depending on the size and length of the water source and/or bridge, and the number of children, you may well split the group for a few different races. If you have time, the children can draw a picture of each stick and write some words to describe it (e.g. smooth/rough, long/short, wide/narrow and branched/unbranched). This step can help with comparing the speeds of different sticks in the water after the race.

You can either use one side of the bridge as the start point and the other side as the finish, or choose a start and finish point in the water for each Poohsticks race. Do a countdown or 'Ready, steady, go!' so the children know when to drop their sticks. For longer stretches of water, you could start, a stopwatch when each race starts and press stop when the first (winning) stick reaches the finish, to give an opportunity to take time measurements.

Repeat the above with more sticks or different objects. You could do a race between sticks and differently shaped objects, such as pine cones. Ask the children to think about why sticks (especially smoother, thinner sticks) are more likely to win Poohsticks than objects with other shapes.

What the children will see

Explain that all objects in water experience water resistance (a type of force that involves friction between the water and the object, slowing the movement of the object down). Some objects will experience less water resistance than others because of their shape: objects that are more streamlined, like long and thin sticks, are likely to move more quickly than bulkier objects or ones that have irregular shapes. The material and surface area of the various objects will also affect how fast they go in a Poohsticks race. If an object has a larger surface area, it will collide more with water particles and therefore have a bigger drag force, slowing it down.

Further ideas for investigation

At the end of the Poohsticks races, the children could create a display of all the competing sticks at the back of the classroom or setting. They could arrange them in order of speed or even create a winner's podium out of different lengths of logs with the first, second and third winning sticks arranged on top.

The children could try making simple boats out of natural materials (e.g. twigs bound together into rafts with long grasses or natural twine) and compare different designs in Poohsticks races. They could even add sails using leaves and try to race them on a windy day.

The hole illusion

The children can use natural materials to learn about how vision works, creating an illusion where they can see through their own hands. This is a short activity that can be used as a starter, or run simultaneously with another activity based around the properties of light and vision.

Links to other activities: 'Shadows and light', 'Sound it out' and 'Picking straws' all discuss light and vision as well as other senses, and use similar materials.

Materials

Required:

- A variety of items to use as straws, such as hollow stems, cardboard tubes, large leaves or scrap paper

Optional:

- Brightly coloured flowers such as daffodils, red roses and orange nasturtiums
- White paper

Activity

Explain to the children that sometimes what we assume is a magic trick is actually all to do with light and how our vision works. Optical illusions deceive our eyes, pretending or seeming to be something they're not. Ask the children each to hold an index finger in front of them (about 30 cm in front of their face) and to keep looking at their finger, but close one eye and then open it and close the other eye (as if winking with their eyes alternately at their finger). Having a background of trees, plants or buildings helps. If winking is difficult for some children, they can use their other hand to close one eye and then the other. What do they notice? Is their finger moving from side to side, or is it the background?

Making a tube

Ask the children to find a straw-like tube, such as a hollow stem, cardboard tube, large leaf or scrap paper rolled into a tube. The children can use this to look through like a telescope. For safety reasons, make sure the children are spread out so that they can't accidentally bump into one another. Also make sure they do not look directly at the Sun on a bright day.

Ask the children each to hold the tube up to one of their eyes whilst closing the other eye, and place their free hand next to the tube, but further away from their closed eye. When both eyes are open, what do the children see?

What the children will see

They should be able to see through their own hands! Well, not really. Explain that this is all to do with binocular fusion: the visual information from each of our eyes is combined with the other's by the brain to make us understand our surroundings as one merged image. This is also why their index fingers would have appeared to move as they winked.

As we humans don't have any natural predators, both our eyes point forwards. Ask the children for examples of animals that are prey and where their eyes are positioned. Explain that animals such as rabbits have eyes on the sides of their heads so they can get a much greater view of what is around them, like a predator waiting to eat them. Right in front of a rabbit's face they have binocular vision like us, where the images from the two eyes combine together. Unfortunately, a predator could catch them from behind, as a rabbit can't see back there. This is why they have amazing ears to hear someone approaching.

Further ideas for investigation

Choose some brightly coloured flowers or plants for the children, making sure ones without or with low pollen are used for hay-fever sufferers (such as those listed above – for more examples please see 'The low allergy garden' leaflet produced by the Royal College of Pathologists, which can be found on their website). Bright yellow, red or orange flowers work well for this. Ask the children to stare at the middle of the flower while slowly counting to 30 in their heads, then ask them to close their eyes. The children could also stare at the coloured flowers placed on white sheets of paper, and then stare at blank sheets of paper instead of closing their eyes.

What do they see when they close their eyes (or look at a blank sheet of paper)? If a yellow flower with a green stalk was used, the children should see a blue flower with a red stalk. Orange and red flowers look green, and blue flowers look red. If a flower's stalk is green, we see a red stalk in the negative image when we close our eyes. But why? Explain that this is because of the opponent process theory of colour vision, and how nerve cells in the visual system (of our eyes and brain) behave. When we stare at a colour for a while, our nerve cells are working very hard to get the information that it is that particular colour. After a while, and as we close our eyes, those nerve cells get tired, but some other nerve cells responsible for giving us information about the opposite colour will work instead, so we see a negative after-image.

Let's pretend

In this creative activity the children will use nature to develop skills in seeing patterns and making connections between them and their wider world.

> **Links to other activities:** 'Remember, remember' and 'Shadows and light' are creative, sensory activities that work well alongside this one, either as part of a longer session or in sequence.

Materials

Required:

- Access to plants in a varied outdoor space, e.g. weeds and moss growing in between paving stones
- Somewhere to view trees, clouds and shadows
- Chalk or charcoal

Optional:

- Mobile phones, tablets or cameras for taking photographs
- Free photo-editing software
- Interactive or dry-erase whiteboard with projector

Activity

The children will often mention explosions, potions and bubbling or fizzing reactions when you ask them what science is all about. Explain to them that there is much more to science than this: that there is a more mindful, thoughtful and creative side too. Scientists often use creative skills to train their power of observation, look at their results in different ways, find patterns when analysing their data and connect up ideas that might seem unconnected. We too can train our brains to be more creative by tapping into our imaginations.

Finding a subject

Ask the children to go outside and find a plant, tree stump, cloud or shadow, or something else outdoors that grabs their attention. Explain that they need to use their imagination to see if they can 'see' anything completely different. Does a cloud look like a dog? Does a shadow look like a dragon? Does a tulip look like it's gossiping with its friends, wafting its leafy arms around?

The children can use chalk or charcoal to draw out what they see on the ground if they're looking at weeds growing in between paving stones or shadows on concrete. Otherwise, the children can try and describe what they see to their peers, and find out if they can see the same thing or something else.

Using technology

Another option is to ask the children to take photos of what they see: a wonky tree stump, a crumpled leaf, a group of small clouds or lichen on a branch. Then bring the group together to try collectively to work out what they can see. If using a tablet with basic editing software installed, perhaps the children can take turns to doodle on the screen what they see (for example, turning the group of clouds into a herd of sheep by adding faces and legs). This can also be done indoors (especially on a wet day, after pictures have been taken earlier) on an interactive or dry-erase whiteboard with the images projected onto it.

Further ideas for investigation

Being able to observe details and describe them effectively are important skills for a scientist. Ask the children what they see when they look really closely. Were there patterns they never noticed before on a flower? Did they see anything else in the moss? Did all the clouds look exactly the same?

The children can work in pairs or small groups for this next part. Ask each pair or group to choose one person to describe something they've found (a flower, leaf, rock, branch etc.) without saying what it is, while the others have their eyes closed. Those listening to the description need to imagine what is being described to them. To make it more difficult, can the describer talk about a flower without mentioning 'petals' and other defining characteristics of a flower?

Without seeing the item, each of the listeners needs to concentrate to try and guess what was being described to them. Was the description good enough to work it out? If not, what words could've been more helpful? Discuss why these skills are useful for scientists doing their research.

Remember, remember

This activity is about developing skills to enable the children to concentrate and focus better. Through these playful, enjoyable outdoor tasks, the children can learn to be more mindful and present, committing their learning to memory.

> **Links to other activities:** Sensory activities such as 'Makes a lot of scents' link well with this activity, as sensory information helps us consolidate our memories.

Materials

- A variety of objects found outdoors or from the classroom (anything from leaves, flowers and twigs to books, pencils and toys)
- A large tablecloth or sheet
- Rocks or bricks (to weigh down the tablecloth or sheet on windy days)

Activity

The process of observation is a valuable skill for scientists, but even more so is the ability to communicate these observations to peers.

I spy

The children will already be familiar with the game 'I spy' but this time, instead of simply guessing, the other children need to ask a question. For example, is it an insect? Does it have leaves? This process of deduction will help the children better understand using keys to identify wildlife.

Memory game

Either choose a set of items or ask the children to find an object each. These could be anything from flowers, pinecones and twigs to classroom objects such as stationery items, toys and books. Place the variety of objects on the ground, and explain each object to the children. If the children chose the objects, perhaps they can explain to the group what each one is. The rest of the group can ask questions about each object too.

Cover all the items with a large tablecloth or sheet (which may need weighing down with rocks or bricks if it is a windy day). Ask all the children to close their eyes, and move items around, add one or take one away. The children need to work out what is different.

To make it a little more difficult (for older groups), ask the children to place the objects around the outdoor space. For example, a book could be placed under a tree. The group then wanders around looking for all the objects without moving them. Collect all the items at the end and show each item, asking the children, 'Where was this object hiding?' Can they associate each object with the hiding place?

Tell me a story

An alternative activity, and this one is linked to circle-time games so there's no need to actually collect objects: ask the children, as individuals or in pairs, to go out and explore something happening in the outdoor space. It could be a ladybird wandering on a leaf, an ant collecting food, a dandelion seed blowing in the wind or a caterpillar crawling up a tree. The children need to remember what they saw and describe it in a sentence as part of a story. Ask one child or pair to begin: 'Once upon a time, there was a shiny red ladybird munching an aphid on a leaf'. Then the next child or pair has to repeat that, and then add their sentence: 'Once upon a time, there was a shiny red ladybird munching an aphid on a leaf, who came across a tiny ant who was collecting food to take back to the nest'.

The story gets longer as the children build it, remembering each other's sentences. They can be as long or short as you like, and it doesn't matter if the children don't all remember everything, as that's part of the brain exercise. Can other children join in and help if anyone forgets a sentence?

What the children will see

Simple games like these can help the children use observation, association, creativity and words to help them remember what they are learning about. Our brains make neural connections in such wonderful ways, committing everything to memory through complex sensory associations. This is why cross-curricular learning can help children of all ages and abilities to make connections and remember what they need to know, with little stress and maximum enjoyment.

Further ideas for investigation

Find out from the children if they've ever learned a valuable lesson from nature, maybe from watching wildlife outdoors. Perhaps they've seen a parent sparrow feeding their chick, a fox cub learning to pounce on its prey or a bumblebee not being the slightest bit distracted while collecting nectar from several flowers. Ask the children to observe some wildlife in the outdoor space. What do they see? What do they think they can learn from these behaviours?

Explain that this is what behavioural scientists and ecologists do. They study individual creatures to find out how they behave and what they do. Although there are behaviours common to all individuals in a species, we each have our own personalities, talents and behaviours. For example, all slugs move the same way, but maybe some individuals are faster or slower, or get more distracted by their surroundings. Seeing these differences in wildlife too can be fascinating to study.

What on earth?

Discover the secret world of soil and why it is so important with these sensory and investigative activities.

> **Links to other activities:** Other biodiversity activities include 'Bioblitz investigation' and 'Plants vs. pests'. 'Wonderful world of worms' also works well alongside this one, as it includes discussions around decomposition of organic material by worms in the soil.

Materials

Required:

- Small spades or shovels
- Soil samples from a few different locations in an outdoor space, which the children can collect during the activity or you can collect in advance, especially if access to outdoor space is limited
- Seed trays or similar containers
- Labels and pens
- Hand lenses

Optional:

- Some examples of inorganic material commonly found in soil, e.g. sand, clay, gravel, rocks and stones

Activity

You can start or end this activity with a quick discussion about what soils do to help us and other living things. Depending on the age of the children, you might ask for their thoughts or you might have some prompt questions such as: Where do we find soil? Does anything live in soil? What can we use soil for? Lead into the practical activity by asking, 'What is soil?'.

Dig up a small amount of soil at each location, giving each place you've collected soil from a name and writing it on a label. Put each soil sample into a separate tray and attach the relevant label. Take the trays to a sheltered spot outside (or place them on tables back in the classroom if you have limited outdoor space). Ask the children to look at the different soil samples and to describe how they look and feel; they can examine the different samples more closely with hand lenses. What is soil made of?

Tell the children it is made of both living and non-living things. Show them rocks, sand and clay if you have them, to demonstrate examples of non-living things.

Can the children see any tiny minibeasts moving around in the soil samples when they look at them through their hand lenses? They might be able to see some of them without hand lenses – for example, centipedes, worms and woodlice are commonly found in soil in the UK. You can discuss how these tiny creatures help 'make' soil by feeding on small pieces of dead plants and animals. Other living things in soil include microbes, which are so small you can see them only with a special instrument called a microscope. Examples of microbes include bacteria and fungi – they do some important jobs in soil, including helping plants grow better and removing nasty pollutants.

Further ideas for investigation

The children can try growing a plant in a moss-covered soil ball called a kokedama, which originated in Japan but are increasingly popular alternatives to hanging baskets. This offers a great way to get hands on with mud, soil and plants.

Making a kokedama

Materials:

- Peat-free compost
- Collected rainwater
- A plant with roots, such as ivy or cyclamens
- Moss sheets
- Garden twine or string
- Scissors

Method:

1. Mix the compost with some water until it is like a wet cake mix.
2. Make a large ball out of the compost mix and squeeze out any excess water.
3. Take the plant and remove any clumps of soil or compost from around the roots.
4. Split the ball of compost into two halves and reshape the ball around the plant's roots.
5. Wrap the moss sheet around the ball and tie garden twine or string around it. Tie the twine in a knot and then wrap more string and tie more knots until the moss is secure.
6. Leave a long length of string to hang up, cutting to the desired length using scissors.

Music to my ears

This activity encourages the children to understand better how sounds are made. Use their creativity to make musical instruments out of natural items.

> **Links to other activities:** 'Sound it out' and 'Audio trails' are other fun sound-based activities. 'Tendon loving care' demonstrates how tendons work, and the children might like to know the difference between tendons and ligaments (as the latter are discussed in this activity).

Materials

Required:

- A variety of natural items, such as conkers, twigs, logs, seed-pods and dried leaves
- Collected rainwater

Optional:

- Grasses
- String or elastic bands
- Spoons or jars
- Hard objects e.g. dishes, metal lids, plates, aluminium pie dishes, foil, cardboard boxes, empty jars and tins
- Buckets
- A piece of hosepipe

Activity

You may wish to run the 'Sound it out' activity first, or revisit it ahead of this one. Ask the children what they remember about how we hear sounds.

Making a sound

Give the children 5–10 minutes to look for items that can make good sounds. During autumn, there will be access to dried leaves, seed-pods and items that make great noises when shaken together.

Explain that there are musical instruments all around the world made from natural materials. For example, the Cas Cas shaker or Kashaka is a percussion instrument from West Africa, which is simply two small dried gourds (a type of vegetable from the pumpkin family) with the dried seeds still inside. They are knocked together and shaken to create amazing rhythms.

The children might like to use string or elastic bands to hold items together. Then, ask the children to play their 'instruments' and perhaps even create a piece of music together. Can they make high- and low-pitched sounds, and loud and soft sounds?

Let's get grassy

If the children can find slightly wide pieces of grass that are flat and each about 5–6 cm long, they can make grass harmonicas. Other similar-sized pieces of foliage can be used, but make sure they don't contain any toxic sap. Ask the children each to fan their hands out, bringing their thumbs together, so that the joints of their thumbs create a small hole. The blade of grass needs to be held between the thumb joints so that the blade runs down the hole. Ask the children to blow between their thumbs and they should hear a sound.

A handful of raindrops

Ask children to take handfuls (they can also use spoons or even jars) of rainwater and pour them gently onto different natural surfaces such as the concrete ground, dried leaves or grass, or onto hard objects like a bucket, a plate, empty tins or crunched-up aluminium foil. What do the children think of the sounds? What if they release only small droplets of rainwater onto each surface, at different times, from different heights? What can they hear? Can they create a rhythm?

What the children will see

With the grass harmonica, the grass works a bit like our vocal chords. Inside our voice box (or larynx), are muscles and ligaments. The air from our lungs makes them vibrate, creating the sounds that we make when we talk and sing. Ligaments are different from tendons, as they connect bone to bone instead of muscle to bone. The sounds of seeds shaking, sticks being hit on surfaces or rainwater dripping onto a bucket are rhythms that we can hear because the sound waves from these items travel into our ears.

Further ideas for investigation

If the children want to collect some water out of a large bucket to make a larger splash of noise, they could use a piece of hosepipe filled with water, dipped into the bucket to release more water out of the bucket. This is known as siphoning. It is all to do with atmospheric pressure, but ask the children to experiment. They should find that they can empty the bucket only if the bucket (or the hose end inside the bucket) is at a higher level than the other end of the hose outside the bucket. Can this water then be trickled out of the hose onto different levels and surfaces to create music?

Makes a lot of scents

Learn about the sense of smell and how it is linked to our memories. Use smelly plants to create natural pest control.

> **Links to other activities:** 'Remember, remember' also discusses memories and our senses. The activity 'Plants vs. pests' covers more on the scents that can be used to deter pests in the garden.

Materials

Required:

- Access to natural 'smells' outdoors (e.g. leaves, flowers and soil)
- Household 'smells' in jars or as they are (e.g. roses, lavender, olive oil, basil, mint, rosemary, cinnamon or other herbs and spices)

Optional:

- Gravel
- Lettuce plants

Activity

Ask the children to wander about outdoors to find some items they might like to smell (but not necessarily pick), such as leaves, flowers, compost or soil and berries. Other options of smells can be given too, like kitchen herbs and spices. When the leaves of herbs are crushed or rubbed between their fingers, children can release the scent even more. Smells can be shared in pairs or small groups so the children can discuss what they think.

> **Safety note**
> Check if any children in your group have hay fever, and if so use cinnamon and a variety of other spices as this will be a safer option. They can also can help their friends locate items to sniff.

Do you remember?

Can the children compare smells to other items they've smelled before? Ask them if any smells remind them of something, such as a time or place. Explain that smells can bring back memories. For example, sniffing cinnamon can remind us of Christmas, and cut grass can remind us of playing football in a field.

If it's a rainy day, why not ask the children to smell the air while it's raining? 'Petrichor' is the name given to the unique earthy smell when it rains: a mix of water and chemicals in the air and soil.

How do smells link to our memories?

Find out how many children know where their brains are. What do they think the brain does? Feel free to revisit some of the information in the 'Remember, remember' activity here. Ask the children what some smells remind them of. Are there any smells they don't like? Perhaps smelling basil makes them think of pizza, and strawberries of summertime.

Explain that our brains have learned many smells. When we smell something new, the scent wafts into the air and travels to our noses. This causes special areas in our noses to send signals up to our brains to tell us what we can smell or what it smells most like. As these signals also go to other areas of the brain, like the areas important for our memories and emotions, these all become linked. This is why, when we smell something, it can remind us of a particular time or person, or make us feel a certain emotion.

Further ideas for investigation

Smelly plants and natural pest control

Ask the children what they understand about pesticides. Explain that sometimes, when planting crops such as beans, carrots and salad leaves, we find that 'pests' like blackflies (a type of aphid.) carrot flies, slugs and snails like to munch on these plants too. Some gardeners spray harmful chemicals (pesticides) to kill off these pests. However, this means that those helpful creatures who eat the pests (e.g. ladybirds, which like to eat aphids) will also die off as they have no food source, which negatively impacts our biodiversity. After heavy rain, pesticides can also wash away into the wider environment, which scientists believe can have harmful effects on wildlife and our health too.

But don't despair! There are ways to keep pests at bay *and* help the environment. Strong-smelling herbs, spices and oils can be used to deter pests. (See 'Plant vs. pests' for more detail.) Other times, the plants just need to be left alone. For example, carrot flies can smell young carrot seedlings being pulled out of the ground to be transplanted elsewhere, and go and lay their eggs in the roots so the larvae eat up the carrots before we can. The easiest option here is just to leave the carrot seedlings to grow without moving them.

But what about slugs and snails? We can deter them as they don't seem to like slithering on top of rough surfaces. Ask the children to create a fair test to investigate a safe method of slug and snail pest control. They could add gravel around lettuce plants – will gravel deter slugs from reaching the lettuce? Slugs also don't seem to like strong-smelling plants like lavender. Maybe that could work too. Perhaps the children would like to test out their ideas and see.

Incredible edibles

This activity is a great way to discover how plants grow and reproduce. Use the edible flowers of your homegrown plants to think about nutrition for humans and pollinators alike.

> **Links to other activities:** The following activities are also about growing:
>
> - A-maze-ing potatoes
> - Seeds of time
> - Seed-sational
> - Bring in the bees (which also features pollinators and more on plant reproduction)
> - Berry nice.

Materials

Required:

- Seeds of plants with edible flowers (one or a range of these, depending on space and time of year: courgette, viola, nasturtium, borage, cornflower, lavender, primrose and forget-me-not)
- Recycled, plastic or homemade seed trays or plant pots (as in 'Making recycled plant pots' on page 45)
- Peat-free compost
- Large plant pots or access to growing area
- Heavy books (or a flower press if you have one)
- Recycled blotting paper, tissue or kitchen paper
- Homemade cookies or fairy cakes
- White icing (e.g. shop-bought glacé icing, or made by mixing 250 g icing sugar and 30 ml warm water)

Activity

Growing your seedlings

Sow your chosen seeds in your seed trays or plant pots containing compost, following any instructions on the packet about depth of sowing. Encourage the children to check on them and water them regularly. When the plants are ready to be moved, get children involved in moving them to bigger pots or even into a flower-bed, if you have this kind of space at your school or in a garden.

Ask the children to keep a record of how the different stages of the growing plants look by taking photos or drawing pictures of them. These could be displayed as a timeline and added to week by week.

Recording visitors

If the seedlings, plants and flowers get any insect visitors at the various stages, these can be recorded too. When the flowers come out, the children can observe pollinators including bees, flies, wasps, beetles and butterflies feeding from the flowers. You can discuss how plants have adaptations to their flower shapes to attract particular insects. For example, some very open flowers like forget-me-nots can be fed on by a range of different flying insects, as their nectar and pollen can be reached by insects with different-shaped mouths. In contrast, borage flowers can be accessed by only bees or butterflies with very long tongues.

Eating flowers

Tell the children that humans can also eat some flowers, and that they are going to use some of the flowers they have grown to make edible cake or biscuit decorations. Each child can collect up to eight flowers. (If you have grown a range of different plants, they can take one or a couple of each.) Some of these can be added fresh as they are or pressed in advance as decorations for your cakes or cookies.

For those being eaten fresh, encourage the children to describe the taste of the flowers. For example, borage will taste like cucumber. You can talk about how we all know vegetables and fruits that come from plants and trees are good for us, but did the children know that flowers also have vitamins in them? For example, courgette flowers contain high levels of vitamins A and E, which help maintain healthy skin and eyes. Flowers in the genus *viola*, such as pansies and violets, are high in vitamin C, which helps your immune system.

> **Safety note**
>
> Not all plants and flowers are safe to eat, so do make sure the children know this and always to check with an adult before tasting any plants.

Pressing and drying edible flowers

To press the rest of the flowers, open up a heavy book somewhere in the middle or towards the back and then place two sheets of kitchen paper or tissue paper between the pages.

Each child can carefully lay their flowers onto the paper and place another two sheets of paper over the top. Several children can use the same book, just use a different page and take care to not dislodge other children's paper and flowers. Close the book carefully, put it in a warm, dry place such as an airing cupboard and place several other heavy books on top of it. Leave for between two and four weeks to dry out fully.

Decorating bakes with flowers

When the flowers are dried and pressed, the children can use these to decorate cakes or biscuits. If you bake your own, you can even put some of the fresh flowers into the cake mix or biscuit dough. To decorate each biscuit or cake with their pressed flowers, the children can place a blob of white icing onto the cake or biscuit and then carefully add their pressed flower on top.

Further ideas for investigation

If you lack space to grow lots of edible flowers, you can buy ready-grown potted plants and try eating and pressing the flowers. You could also visit a local community garden or similar and help the children collect edible flowers.

If you have a fair bit of space, you could grow courgette plants and eat both the flowers and the fruits (the courgettes). This is a great way to discuss plant reproduction as well as demonstrate the different parts of a plant that we can eat. Courgettes have two types of flower: the flower with a young courgette attached is the female, and the more eye-catching flower (to attract the pollinators) on the long stalk is the male. When the female flower is pollinated, the young courgette will grow into a big one. As the male flowers are a bit useless after the bees have used them for pollinating, we can pick those flowers and eat them. They can be eaten raw or cooked. (Deep-frying them is popular but perhaps not practical with a group of children.) You can pick the female flowers and eat the tiny courgettes or wait until they have grown into bigger courgettes and eat them then.

Seed-sational

Explore the amazing world of seeds with these seed-based activities to help the children better understand our planet's biodiversity.

> **Links to other activities:** The following activities also cover seeds, plants and growing your own food. You might wish to run these as class projects together over spring and early summer terms, or as part of an after-school gardening club.
>
> - Sunflower power
> - Seeds of time
> - Berry nice
> - Incredible edibles
> - Can weeds help us?

As an introduction to these activities, you could encourage the children to search for the seeds in their cupboards, fridges and local gardens or green spaces. Discuss what seeds are and where they are found in a plant. Ask the children if they can think of any seeds we eat (e.g. pumpkin and sunflower seeds) and what other animals might eat seeds – birds and insects are two examples you can use.

Activity

Making seed balls

Materials:

- Peat-free compost or soil
- Flour
- A mixing bowl
- Chilli powder (to deter seed-eating creatures)
- Collected rainwater
- Wildflower seeds
- A tray

Method:

1. To make the wildflower seed balls, mix ten parts soil to one part flour in a bowl.
2. Add a jar of chilli powder (a standard 44 g jar for around 1 kg soil) and water until you have a sticky dough-like consistency.
3. Roll the mixture into balls, around the size of golf balls, and then roll them in a tray of wildflower seeds.
4. Leave them somewhere warm to dry for a couple of days.

Safety note

Take care when using the chilli powder – it can cause you to cough if inhaled, or very sore eyes if you touch your eyes with a little powder on your fingers. It is best if an adult tips the chilli into the ball mixture and does the initial mixing. The children can then handle the dough to make the balls, but ensure they all wash their hands thoroughly and tell them to not touch their eyes.

Seed balls are best 'thrown' (rather than sown) in spring or autumn onto exposed soil, as opposed to grass. Areas of bare soil in urban areas are a great place to try 'seed-bombing' with your balls. Avoid leaving seed balls in nature reserves or protected areas, as these often have specific plant species and are managed carefully by conservationists.

Activity: Sow your spice cupboard

Materials

- Jars of whole spices, e.g. mustard seeds, coriander seeds, cumin seeds, fenugreek seeds, cardamom pods and nutmeg kernels (ideally two years old or less)
- Small recycled plastic or homemade plant pots (as in 'Making recycled plant pots' on page 45)
- Peat-free compost
- Pens
- Wooden lolly sticks
- Small watering cans or similar

> **Teacher tip**
>
> - If using nutmeg kernels, soak them in water around 24 hours before you run this activity – this makes them more likely to germinate.
> - You can eat the leaves of all of the plants listed, although nutmeg and cardamom leaves are best dried first and used to flavour stews and curries.

Look at the seeds collected from your and the children's food cupboards. Have the children seen any of them used in cooking? Talk about how they come from different plants and that's why they look and smell so differently from each other.

Ask the children to put compost in the pots, up to about two thirds from the tops. They can use one pot for each type of spice seed they're growing. Ask them to write the name of each of the spices on one of four separate lolly sticks and place one into each pot. Then hand around the seeds. Each child can sprinkle a few of each seed onto the compost, except in the case of nutmeg where they will need only one each. Then ask the children to cover the seeds over with more compost and then give each pot some water. Place the pots in a sunny spot such as a windowsill, greenhouse or similar to start with, and then transfer outside if possible, and water whenever they look a bit dry.

Encourage the children to record the different stages of growth of each type of spice seed. Talk about how some of them might grow better or faster than others because of where they come from in the world. For example, cumin originates from West Africa where it is much hotter than the UK. Mustard, on the other hand, originates from high in the Himalayas where it is much colder. Nutmeg is not actually a nut but rather a seed of the Myristica plant, which is native to the Banda Islands, a small cluster of islands in Indonesia. The fruit of a nutmeg plant is golden and looks a bit like an apricot. The edible part of the seed inside a nutmeg's fruit is where the spices nutmeg and mace come from. These spices are used in lots of delicious sweet and savoury recipes, including soups and hot cross buns.

A few weeks later, when the plants have grown a few leafy stems, encourage the children to try the fresh leaves of coriander, cumin, fenugreek and mustard and describe the taste. Talk about why plants have leaves that taste and smell strong or bitter. This is to try and deter herbivorous insects such as beetles. Mustard is a good example: the tangy taste a mustard plant develops discourages insect predators – this can be the difference between life and death for the plants.

Further ideas for investigation

Discuss with the children why wildflowers are so important for biodiversity, bees and supporting our local environments. Encourage the children to search for wildflowers in their local parks and green spaces. Maybe they would like to do a research project and present on their favourite local wildflowers. Investigate opportunities to get the children involved in wildflower-planting initiatives in local public spaces, or set up your own mini wildflower patch in pots or small unused spaces around your school.

Making seed postcards

Materials:

- Used paper
- Jars
- Fabric (for soaking up water)
- Paintbrushes
- Paints or natural dyes (as in 'Paint with nature' on page 86)

Method:

1. Tear the used paper into tiny pieces.
2. Put the paper into a jar, add some water and give it a good shake.
3. Leave the jar for a few days, shaking it every day to break up the paper fibres, eventually creating a pulp.
4. Tip the paper pulp out onto some fabric, and form a postcard shape.
5. Add the seeds and add more pulp on top.
6. Put another piece of material on top and squeeze as much of the water out of the paper pulp as possible. (You can do this outside or over the sink.) Leave it all to dry in a sunny spot.
7. When the postcard is fully dry, use ready-made paints or natural dyes and paint a design on the front.
8. To grow their seed-embedded postcard, children can simply put it in a pot with some compost or soil (they can tear it into small pieces first) and then put some more compost on top of it and water regularly.

Paint with nature

These simple activities offer a way for the children to experiment with painting using natural materials including natural dyes, feather paintbrushes and printing with leaves.

> **Links to other activities:** Other activities that cover natural fashion, colours and dyes include 'Wear on earth', 'Changing colours' and 'Feather forecast'. You can link the 'Leaf printing' activity to others involving discussions about photosynthesis, such as 'Sunflower power' and 'A-maze-ing potatoes'.

Activity: Natural dyes

Materials

- Marigold or rose petals
- Three large heatproof bowls
- Boiling water
- Wooden lollipop sticks
- Bicarbonate of soda
- White vinegar
- Paper
- Paintbrushes

> **Safety note**
> This activity works best as a demonstration because boiling water is involved.

Take the petals and drop them into the first bowl. It is best to stick to petals of one colour per bowl so you can compare the effect of acid vs. alkali. You could always repeat the experiment with petals of other colours in additional bowls.

Pour boiling water over the petals – just enough so the petals are covered. Do the same with two other bowls and then use your wooden lollipop sticks to mix the petals in the water. The water will change colour right away, but will continue to darken for a while longer.

In the first bowl, add a sprinkle of bicarbonate of soda. The alkaline (or basic) pH of the bicarbonate of soda will shift the colour to a darker orangey red. Pour some vinegar into the second bowl. The acid will make the colour very bright. Leave the third bowl as it is, containing just petals and water. These are the three dyes.

Once the dyes have cooled down to room temperature, the children can try painting with the different-coloured dyes. You can discuss how adding the alkaline bicarbonate of soda made the dye go darker and how the acid vinegar made it go brighter. See 'Changing colours' for more information about pH and plant indicators.

Activity: Feather paintbrushes

Materials

- Collected feathers
- Twigs, dowels or wooden pencils
- Recycled paper tape
- Paints or natural dyes (as in the 'Natural dyes' activity on page 86)
- Paper

> **Safety note**
> Ensure the children wash their hands thoroughly before and after this activity.

The best time to do this is late summer when birds are moulting. The children could be encouraged to collect feathers over the summer holidays.

First ask the children to look at the different types of collected feathers and think about how they look and feel. Why do birds have feathers? And why do they lose some of them in the summer? A feather is a 'dead' structure, like hair or nails in humans, and is made of the protein keratin. Just like we lose some of our hairs and grow more (unless we have a condition or are going bald), birds also lose some of their older feathers and grow new ones. The process of losing some old feathers so they can be replaced with new ones is called moulting. Talk about how feathers can be different colours to help birds camouflage themselves in different habitats and how they keep birds warm in colder months.

Ask the children to think about which of the feathers might work best as paintbrushes. They can try using the feathers as paintbrushes on their own, or gather a few together and tape them to a pencil, twig or piece of doweling to make a larger paintbrush. You could get a large roll of paper and the children could use their feather paintbrushes to paint an art-science display jointly about birds and their feathers. If you try making the natural dyes from petals (as in the 'Natural dyes' activity on page 86), the children could using their feather paintbrushes to paint with them.

Activity: Leaf printing

Materials

- Collected leaves (ideally including ferns, which are particularly good for this activity)
- Scrap material, e.g. plain tote bags, pillow cases or old sheets cut into smaller pieces
- A wooden board, bench or other hard surface
- Small wooden mallets, pebbles or stones (suitable for the children to hold in one hand)
- Soya milk (optional)

The best time for this activity is early summer when leaves are young. Run this activity soon after you've collected the leaves. Ensure the children don't collect too many leaves from one particular area of a tree, bush or plant – they need only four or five different leaves for each fabric item they're going to print on.

Before they start printing, discuss with the children what different shapes of leaves they have collected and what leaves are for. Leaves are the part of the plant where photosynthesis takes place. Photosynthesis is the process plants go through to make food, by using sunlight and chlorophyll to turn water and carbon dioxide into nutrients.

> **Fact file: Leaf shapes**
>
> Different plants have different-shaped leaves, depending on the environment they evolved in. Rounder leaves (like beech or lime), are more efficient at absorbing sunlight but are also more prone to wind damage, so rounder leaves tend to be smaller than broader leaves. Larger leaves tend to be lobed or cut (like oak and maple), because their shape is better able to withstand the wind. Leaves of trees from colder climates, like pine trees, are needle-shaped. This shape has reduced surface area and therefore a reduced risk of freeze damage. Leaves at no risk of freeze damage tend to be large, such as tropical palm leaves.

> **Teacher tip**
>
> It can work well for the children to work in pairs on this activity: this reduces the number of leaves being collected from growing plants and also the space needed to set up the activity.

To make each leaf-printed piece of fabric, place the first leaf underneath the fabric where you want the print of it to appear. Gently bash the leaf through the fabric using the wooden mallet or rock until it is 'crushed' onto the fabric. Peel off the crushed leaf from the underside of the fabric and then repeat with the rest of the leaves until you have created your print. This method is best for making decorative pieces that don't require repeated washing. Some leaf pigments will withstand machine washing more than others, and all will fade naturally over time anyway. If you do want to make a garment or something that you will wash more, consider pre-treating the fabric by soaking it in soya milk overnight – this will help bind the pigments to the fabric.

Further ideas and investigation

Mix and match the activities. Try the leaf-printing activity using flowers instead. Why not try mixing different coloured flower dyes to see what colours you can make? These activities work well in cross-curricular lessons with art and design and technology.

Section 3

How are we linked to nature?

Reduce; reuse; recycle

These activities can aid the children's understanding of the impact of our everyday lives on the environment, breaking down why we need to recycle and compost.

> **Links to other activities:** The following activities contain elements of this activity and would be nice to revisit with your group (involving topics that include reusing, heat, insulation, growing and composting):
>
> - Circle of influence
> - The heat is on
> - Feather forecast
> - Berry nice.

Materials

Required:

- Range of items to be sorted (cleaned if necessary), including:
  - packaging – plastic containers, scrap paper, cardboard packaging, metal tins, cans
  - items of clothing made of natural and non-natural fibres – cotton T-shirts, fleeces, woollen scarves, bamboo socks, plastic shoes
  - fresh food items – apples, bananas, bread, potatoes, other fruits and vegetables
- Two large containers labelled 'biodegradable' and 'not biodegradable' (such as storage boxes without lids or sturdy cardboard boxes)
- Glass jars (the larger the better)
- Soil
- Food scraps, e.g. banana skins, apple cores and orange peelings (perhaps collected after break time or after the children have eaten fruit you provided at the start of the session)

Optional:

- Grass clippings
- Biodegradable food waste bags
- Cardboard scraps

Activity

Introductory discussion

Most of us are familiar with separating out our rubbish for recycling, but how can we reduce the amount of rubbish we create in the first place? And what does 'biodegradeable' mean?

Ask the children if they have ever heard the term 'biodegradable'. Explain that this is a word used to describe objects and materials that can be broken down (decomposed) by living things, including invertebrates such as worms, microbes such as bacteria, and fungi. Once a biodegradable thing has been broken down in this way and mixed with other things in nature, it essentially becomes soil and can be used for growing new plants like trees, vegetables and fruit.

If something is *not* biodegradable, that means it can't be broken down in this way and can cause problems in our environment. For example, plastic carrier bags from supermarkets end up in rivers and woods and, because they can't be broken down by the bacteria and fungi that live there, this causes harm to wildlife such as birds and fish. This is why many people take reusable bags to get their supermarket shopping. However, there still are lots of things we buy every day that come packaged in non-biodegradable materials like plastic.

Sorting waste

Ask the children to sort the fresh and waste items you've provided (excluding the food scraps, which are a bit messy and can be saved for the second part of this activity) into the correct box. Encourage them to think about what each item might be made of and if bacteria are likely to be able to break it down. You could give them extra facts for certain items like 'these socks are made of bamboo, which is a plant' and 'this corrugated cardboard is made of trees', etc.

Ask the children to think about what will happen to all of the non-biodegradable, which once they're thrown away. Those that we put in our recycling might be turned into something new, but first they have to be shredded or melted. This all uses even more energy, so it would be better to reuse the plastic containers (e.g. make them into flower pots) or buy fewer things that are made of or packaged in plastic (e.g. buy fruit and vegetables that are 'loose').

Composting experiment

Tell the children they are going to start a composting experiment to see how long biodegradable waste takes to decompose. Give each pair or group of children an empty glass jar and ask them to put a layer of soil at the bottom, followed by a layer of grass clippings (optional). Then they can add their fruit peelings followed by another layer of soil (plus additional layers of food waste, depending on the size of the jar). They might also like to add one biodegradable food-waste bag or some small pieces of cardboard to see how quickly these break down. Don't put a lid or covering on these composting jars – allow oxygen in to avoid them becoming anaerobic and smelly.

Explain to the children that bacteria, worms and other living things that are naturally in the soil will start to 'eat' the food waste and turn it into something that looks like the compost you see in garden centres and potted plants. Discuss what might speed up or slow down this process. For example, ask the children to predict what will happen if some of the jars are placed in a sunny location and some are placed in a dark, shady location. Heat energy can increase the number of bacteria in the jar (as they will grow and divide to make new bacteria more quickly), speeding up the rate that the food-waste items are broken down.

The children can make observations of their jars over the next few weeks and even keep a photo or picture record of what is happening to the waste. Once the food waste has become compost, the children can transfer the material into plant pots (perhaps using some of the plastic waste items from the waste-sorting activity) and try growing a new plant (as in the 'Berry nice' activity below).

Further ideas for investigation

You could add a second stage to the waste-sorting activity by sorting the non-biodegradable waste products into recyclable and non-recyclable so children can think about where the rubbish in their bin might end up (i.e. in landfill).

Berry nice

Growing food is a great way to teach young people about the process of where our food comes from. This activity shows the children how to grow plants from kitchen scraps, and learn about the ways in which different plants grow. This activity works well in the summer, when it's warm and strawberries are in season.

> **Links to other activities:** The following activities also cover growing and learning about seeds: 'A-maze-ing potatoes', 'Seeds of time', 'Sunflower power' and 'Seed-sational'.

Materials

Required:

- Strawberries
- Small bowls
- A fine-meshed sieve
- Kitchen roll or a tea towel
- Small recycled plastic or homemade plant pots (as in 'Making recycled plant pots' on page 45)
- Peat-free compost
- Pencils

Optional:

- Forks or potato mashers
- Food scraps (e.g. tomatoes, potatoes, sunflowers, carrots, beetroot)
- Plant cuttings (e.g. basil, garlic)
- Various seeds (e.g. beetroot, spinach, chilli, aubergine)

Activity

> **Fact file: Strawberries**
>
> A single strawberry can have as many as 200 seeds. Strawberries are an excellent source of vitamins C and K, and also contain fibre, folic acid, manganese and potassium.
>
> Sometimes gardeners and farmers place a lot of straw around strawberry plants to keep the fruit dry so they won't touch the wet soil and rot. This also helps stop weeds competing with the plants, using up water and nutrients in the soil. This is why they are called 'straw-berries'!

Growing strawberries

Show the children some strawberries, and explain that strawberries are fruits that have all their seeds on the outside. Ask the children to remove the green tops from a couple of strawberries, place the strawberries in a bowl with some water and squish the flesh into small pieces using their fingers, forks or potato mashers.

The children can then pour the strawberry pulp into a sieve with very small holes and rinse the pulp with a little water, so they have only the seeds left. Ask them to spread the seeds onto a couple of sheets of kitchen roll and leave them on the side to dry out.

Once the seeds have dried (possibly after a few days), ask the children to remove the seeds from the kitchen roll gently. Prepare a small plant pot of compost that has been watered. The children can sprinkle some of their strawberry seeds onto the surface, cover with a little more compost and sprinkle more water on top.

What the children will see

Explain that the first part of the strawberry plant (and most plants) to grow is the shoot, with two baby leaves called cotyledons. Gradually more leaves will start to appear and, as they grow, the plants may need repotting. The children can repot them into bigger pots or, if it's warm outdoors, these can be planted directly into the ground in a sunny spot. If you're using recycled cardboard plant pots, these can be planted directly into the bigger pot as the material will decompose.

If you're using small plant pots, ask the children to take each strawberry plant out of the pot carefully, making sure the stem and roots are still attached to each other. They can then each use a pencil to create a hole in the soil they're transferring to, so that the roots of the plant are placed into the hole. Then they can fill in the space around the plant's shoot with compost. If this is directly in the ground or a large container, they can plant the next seedling at least 2.5 cm away. Plants can be kept inside until flowers appear and should be watered regularly.

As soon as the children see white flowers with yellow centres appear on their strawberry plants, it's time to take the plants outside for bees and butterflies to visit. After pollination, whitish green fruits will appear, and then turn red as they ripen in the Sun. They will be ready to harvest (and eat) when they are bright red and smelling delicious.

More food to grow from scraps

Ask the children what other vegetables, fruits or flowers they would like to grow using scraps and leftover food that might otherwise go to waste. Which of these would the children like to try growing next?

- Tomatoes: Seeds harvested from a supermarket-bought tomato can be used to grow tomato plants using the same method as in the activity.
- Carrots and beetroot: Place the tops into a shallow dish of water or jar lid and watch them sprout edible greens out the top.
- Spices: Mustard, coriander and fenugreek seeds from the spice cupboard can all be planted in pots of compost to grow cress-like microgreens.
- Potatoes: When potatoes start sprouting or chitting, which is when short buds (or eyes) start to sprout out of them, they can be planted too. Plant these seeding potatoes in a bucket of compost or directly in the ground. Potatoes aren't very fussy and will grow in no time. See 'A-maze-ing potatoes' for a fun activity demonstrating this.
- Flowers: Take the seeds from a sunflower (for example) to eat, feed to birds or plant to grow more sunflowers.

Further ideas for investigation

Discuss what the children have learned about growing their own food from scraps and things they can find at home. Explain that food waste is a huge problem in the Global North. It is thought to cost billions of pounds in the UK and account for around 8 per cent of our greenhouse gas emissions every year. What have the children learned about how to reduce food waste at home?

Growing plants from runners

Sometimes strawberries create seeds that don't germinate or grow into full plants because the seeds aren't mature, they're taking too long to germinate or the growing conditions aren't quite right. The children could experiment with shop-bought seeds too to grow more new plants, but strawberries are renowned for growing runners. This is where a small 'child' plant sprouts from the 'parent' plant. These small strawberry plants have teeny roots that can be pushed into some compost and grown into large plants.

Growing plants from cuttings and bulbs

Older children may be interested in growing plants from cuttings, such as taking a stalk from a shop-bought basil plant and putting it into a glass of water. The stalk should have a couple of leaves at the top above the water level and at least one leaf node (where the leaves further down have been removed) submerged in the water. Roots will soon appear at the leaf node. The children might also be interested in how garlic grows: each clove from one garlic bulb can be planted to grow more bulbs.

Comparing seeds

Seeds are fascinating in themselves and reveal a lot of clues as to how the plants they end up as are related. For example, show the children a variety of seeds, such as from tomatoes and aubergines, and ask them to compare them to beetroot and spinach seeds. They should find that the former look similar to one another as they're from the same botanical family. The latter look similar to each other as they're related, but tomato seeds look very different from beetroot seeds. The children can learn about classification and taxonomy through simply studying seeds.

Bring in the bees

This is an investigation into nature's buzziest insects. The children will find out why bees buzz in and out of flowers and how the two help each other.

> **Links to other activities:** The following activities also cover biodiversity and pollinators: 'Bioblitz investigation', 'Wildlife needs you' and 'Can weeds help us?'. 'Incredible edibles' also covers growing food.

Materials

- Some insect-pollinated fruits and vegetables, e.g. apples, pears, blueberries, strawberries, beans, courgettes or tomatoes
- An area of flowering plants (ideally with more than one type of flowering plant in it), e.g. a hedgerow, a flower-bed or potted plants
- Pollinator identification sheets, enough for one per group (which can be downloaded from a range of reliable organisations including Buglife and the Natural History Museum)
- Pencils
- Transparent bug pots, or glass jars and discs of paper or cloth with pin-holes in them, to use as breathable lids
- Flowering tomato plants
- Insect-bite cream and antihistamines

Activity

Why are bees important?

Ask the children if they know what bees do for humans. They may or may not know that they pollinate lots of the plants we eat. They might also answer that 'bees make honey'. Start to talk about bees' involvement in growing fruits and vegetables we eat, and pass around the examples you've brought in. If you have the means, it can be a nice addition to cut up some of the fruits and vegetables for the children to taste. Tell the children that bees are a type of pollinator and many plants rely on bees and other insects to produce fruits. If we didn't have bees, we wouldn't be able to grow as many of the lovely fruits and vegetables we eat today.

Ask the children where they are most likely to see bees when they're in a garden or park. Hopefully they will be able to tell you they have spotted bees on flowers. You can explain that, before plants produce fruits, they produce flowers. The flowers are often brightly coloured and pleasantly scented to attract insects like bees. They also produce a sugary substance called nectar – this is what bees like to eat.

Bees also collect something from the plant called pollen, which is made by the male parts of a flower: the stamens and anther. The pollen sticks to the bee's hairy legs and body. When the bee visits the next flower, some of the pollen rubs off the bee onto the female part of the flower, which is called the stigma (the top part of the pistil, which also contains the ovary and ovule). Once the flower is fertilised, it will lose its petals and the ovary will swell up and turn into a delicious fruit. This is how plants reproduce.

Tell the children that they are going to spot different types of pollinators and use some identification sheets to record which ones, and how many, they see. Some will be bees and some will be other insects. Ask the children if they can think of some other flying insects. Lots of the ones they know (e.g. butterflies, beetles and flies) also act as pollinators; it is not just bees that pollinate.

> **Safety note**
>
> We recommend having an EpiPen® on site with a First Aider who is trained in using it for this activity. Even if none of the children or adults has known allergies to bee or wasp stings, severe allergic reactions can occur suddenly without any previous episodes.

Pollinator observations

This activity works best on a sunny day when it's not too windy. Before the children start recording pollinators, try and catch a couple of examples in a pot or jar for them to look at to get familiar with the differences between them. Bees and beetles feeding from flowers are fairly easy to catch in a pot for a short amount of time; hoverflies are less easy and it is best to avoid trying to catch butterflies as they are easily damaged.

Show the children any pollinators you're able to catch and ask them to describe them, e.g. whether they have hairy bodies and wings. You can help the children spot bees vs. other striped flying insects by pointing out that bees have two pairs of wings (four in total). You can also highlight the fact that honeybees are less hairy than bumblebees and that there are lots of different types of bees, including quite small ones that can be easily missed. Make sure you release any insects you've captured in jars or pots after ten minutes or so.

Give the children a pollinator ID sheet and a pencil and ask them to spread out around the flowering area so they're all observing different flowers. They could keep a tally against the different types of pollinators on the ID sheet you're using. If there are different colours and shapes of flowers, you could also encourage them to observe if some flower types are preferred by one or more types of pollinator. This can lead into conversations about how plants have evolved different shapes of flowers to attract different pollinators. (See 'Incredible edibles' for more on this.)

After 20 minutes or so, gather the group back together and see what they've observed collectively. Ask them if they saw any pollen sticking to any of the pollinators and if they noticed them flying between lots of different flowers of the same plant species. Bees are particularly effective pollinators because of how hairy they are. They can also be very 'loyal' to one type of plant, meaning the plant can guarantee pollination if the right kind of bee is around. You can also explain that bees also keep some of the pollen for themselves: they make it into a special protein and vitamin-rich food called pollen bread, and feed it to baby bees (larvae).

Tomato-plant pollination

Use some flowering tomato plants to extend learning about the link between insect pollination and human food. Explain to the children that the little yellow flowers they see on the tomato plants will turn into tomatoes that we can eat. While tomatoes can self-pollinate in glasshouses, bee pollination is more effective and will ensure lots of large and juicy tomatoes.

Set up a rota for different children to spend ten minutes per day observing the tomato plants in a sunny spot. Ask them to record the numbers of bees and other pollinators they see visiting the yellow flowers. If possible, they could try to identify them using an ID sheet, or simply the broad group they fit into (e.g. honeybees, bumblebees, small or solitary bees, flies, butterflies, etc.).

The pollen in tomato flowers is packed tightly into the anther. Most insects are unable to access this pollen, but bumblebees are able to create strong vibrations by contracting their flight muscles, leading to an explosion of pollen grains from the tip of the anther – this is also known as 'buzz pollination'. The bee will comb most of these pollen grains from its fur and into the pollen baskets on its hind legs. A few pollen grains will be missed and will go on to fertilise some of the next flowers it visits.

Blueberries, tomatoes, aubergines and kiwis are just some examples of the many plant species that benefit from this form of pollination. These plants have evolved tightly packed pollen in their anthers, to reduce the amount of pollen that is lost to inefficient pollinators and 'pollen thieves'. Bumblebees have evolved this ability to 'explode' the tightly packed pollen out of these plants' flowers, giving them an advantage in accessing the protein-rich pollen that their competitors can't access. Bumblebees are so good at buzz pollination that they are sometimes 'employed' by commercial tomato growers, who release them into huge glasshouses to pollinate their tomato crops.

After all of the tomato-plant flowers are pollinated, the children can observe the next stages of the plant's life cycle and hopefully then enjoy some delicious tomatoes.

Further ideas for investigation

You could repeat the pollinator-observation activity in different areas or sites in your local vicinity. Create a pollinator map for the classroom wall to show the different pollinators the children have observed in different areas of the school, garden or local area.

In early-education settings, you could run a 'be a bee' activity, involving the children going around a garden or park trying to spot as many different colours of flowers as they can, ticking them off a sheet according to each colour.

Wildlife needs you

This set of complementary activities offers an engaging way for the children to learn about the impacts of humans on the natural environment and create welcoming spaces for your local wildlife.

No matter how small or limited your outdoor space is, there are easy ways you can encourage more wildlife into it. These activities can get the children thinking about habitats and what animals need to survive.

> **Links to other activities:** The following activities all cover observing wildlife in our local areas:
> - The wonderful world of worms
> - What was here before us?
> - Can weeds help us?
> - Bring in the bees.

Activity

Loo-roll bird feeders

Materials:

- Bird seed
- Reusable plates or shallow plant pots
- Loo-roll tubes
- String
- Safety scissors
- Small spatulas or wooden rounded pallet knives
- A few jars of peanut butter or lard (or nut-free, plant-based alternative)

Method:

1. Spread the bird seed out on a plate.
2. Cut a 30–50 cm piece of string using the safety scissors and set it aside.
3. Use a spatula to spread peanut butter (or alternative) on the outside of the loo-roll tube.
4. Gently roll it in the seeds so they stick to the peanut butter (or alternative).
5. Thread the string through the tube, tie a knot and hang it in a tree or similar.

You could compare different bird-seed mixes to see which birds prefer different types of seeds. For example, small seeds, such as millet, are loved by house sparrows, dunnocks, finches, reed buntings and collared doves, while flaked maize is enjoyed by blackbirds. Tits and greenfinches love sunflower hearts, peanuts and sunflower seeds. The RSPB's Big Schools' Birdwatch resource sheets will help children identify and record common bird species they see munching on their feeders. (www.rspb.org.uk/whats-happening/get-ready-for-big-schools-birdwatch/resources)

Activity: Beetle bucket

Materials

- A bucket, trug or other durable, upcycled container
- A small craft knife (for grown-up use only)
- Spades or large trowels
- Small logs or branches (which will fit upright in your container)
- Stones, bark chips and leaves

Fact file: Beetles

One fun fact about beetles is that there are over 4,000 species of them in the UK alone. Many of them do helpful jobs like eating dead plant material and pollinating flowers. Others are useful food for hedgehogs, badgers, birds and other animals. Lots of beetles like to live in damp places low to the ground.

Before the session, use the craft knife to create some 3 cm holes in the sides and bottom of your bucket: these are to allow beetles to enter and exit your bucket habitat. Also find a suitable spot for the bucket: somewhere quiet and out of sight is best, and ensure the ground is suitable for digging. Water the ground regularly over a few days in advance of the session if you're worried it will be too hard to dig.

Introduce the session by asking the children if they can name any types of beetle. They will have likely heard of stag beetles, but do they know any others? Tell the children that they are going to make a beetle habitat using a bucket sunk into the ground.

Divide the children up into different teams (two or three depending on the number of children in the group). One team can help dig a hole big enough for the prepared bucket, another can collect small logs that are large enough to stand up inside the bucket and the last team can collect dead leaves, bark chips and stones in a variety of sizes.

The first team needs to make sure the hole is just bigger than the bucket. They could measure its circumference first and then mark a circle slightly larger than that where they can then dig. Once the hole is big enough (possibly after you step in and help dig out some big chunks if time is limited), place the bucket inside.

Ask the children to place some stones at the bottom of the bucket, followed by a few logs that should be arranged so they're standing upright, leaning against the side of the bucket. After this add leaves, bark and any other natural materials the children have collected. Leave around 10 cm at the top and fill this in with some of the soil you dug out from the ground. You can place a few more logs over the top of the hole to mark the spot and to encourage other beetles and wildlife to visit.

After a couple of weeks, you can go on a beetle hunt. Carefully dig through the top layer of your beetle bucket and record the different beetles you see. Remember to replace the soil and logs after each beetle hunt.

Activity: Mini insect hotels

Materials

- Corrugated cardboard cut into 40 x 20 cm strips, or large plastic bottles (each cut into a cylinder, with sharp edges made safe with wide tape)
- Scissors
- Recycled paper tape
- A variety of natural items such as pine cones, bark, pieces of moss, sticks and twigs (and any other natural materials you can collect that will create nooks and crannies for bugs to hide in)
- Bamboo or similar natural straws (detailed in 'Picking straws' on page 119).
- String

> **Teacher tip**
>
> If using plastic bottles, cut them down to cylinders in advance of the session (as this can take up too much time and involves lots of scissor supervision). If using corrugated cardboard, cut this into strips approximately 40 cm high by 20 cm wide, roll these up into loose tubes and secure with tape. They will become more stable and rigid when stuffed with insect nesting material.

If you can, get the children to collect some of the materials for their mini insect hotels at the start of the session. Get them to think about what kinds of material would make the best homes for insects. You can show them the bamboo and explain that insects like small bees look for holes and tube-like places to build their nests. Others, like ladybirds, prefer bundles of twigs that create small crevices where they can keep warm over winter, while earwigs like dried grass or straw to hide in – so it's good to have a few different types of natural material in your insect hotels. If the children collect dead leaves, you could create a pile of them somewhere separate: they're not as useful for the insect hotels but they can provide a great hibernation spot for hedgehogs, frogs, toads and various other animals.

Encourage the children to arrange the materials they've collected by size and texture, and to think about the size of twigs they will need for their insect hotels so they can start to snap the twigs down to the right size. You can demonstrate the stuffing process to the children before they each start their own, showing how to layer up the different materials, starting with the sturdiest and most uniform items (i.e. the bamboo) and then adding the twigs followed by the pine cones, moss and other materials. Encourage the children to make their hotels nice and cosy by stuffing them full, so bits don't fall out.

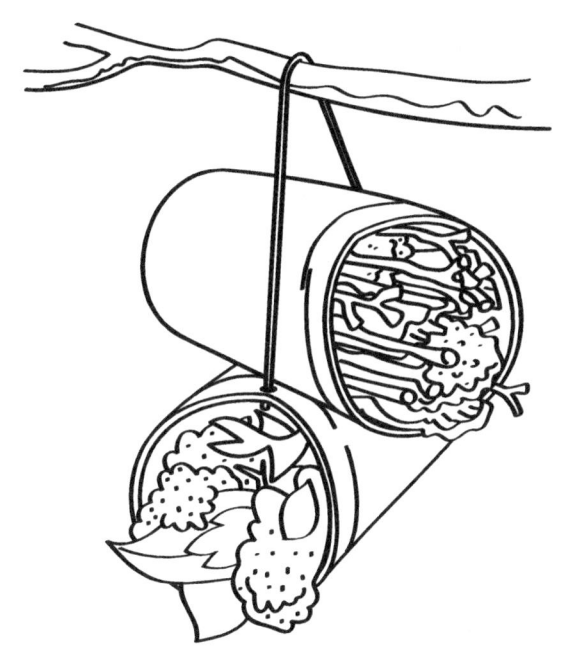

Give them each some twine or string so they can tie this around the bottle or cardboard tube, leaving enough length for hanging up the insect hotel later. Some of the children might have places outside their homes where they could hang them up. For those who don't, encourage them to pick spots for hanging their insect hotels around the school grounds. You could also have some children placing their hotels on the ground, as a way of comparing the different insects that might be attracted at different heights.

Leave the insect hotels in different locations as mentioned, outside the children's homes or in a few different spots around the school grounds. You could also encourage the children to offer them to local outdoor spaces in your community, such as the grounds of village halls or community centres, allotments, churchyards, and even café and pub gardens. After a few months, have a look at what is living in the different insect hotels. The children could create a map of the different wildlife found in different locations in their school or local area.

Activity: Cardboard hedgehog homes

> ### Fact file: Hedgehog habitats
>
> Hedgehogs are common in most areas of the UK apart from moorlands, pine forests and uplands. They can be found living in both the countryside and urban areas. While their preferred habitats are hedgerows and the edges of woodlands, urban gardens with plants and shrubs can provide excellent habitats and food for hedgehogs. Making a hedgehog home in a school garden could give a local hedgehog a more-secure place to shelter and breed. If you don't have any green space on site, you could try contacting your local community garden, park or nature reserve to see if they would allow you to set up a hedgehog home at their site. Obviously, taking the children off-site can involve a fair amount of resources and planning, so may not be an option for everyone.

Materials

Required:

- A sturdy, medium-sized cardboard box (shoebox size is ideal)
- A craft knife
- Logs, bits of bark, twigs, leaves and grass

Optional:

- Hedgehog food
- Dog or cat food

In advance of the session, turn your box upside down and cut a 15 x 15 cm 'doorway' (hole) in the front. Cut some small air holes into the side of your hedgehog home so it doesn't get too damp inside.

Have a look at your outdoor space and discuss with the children where the best place for the hedgehog home would be. Explain that the best place would be alongside a fence as hedgehogs tend to walk along fences to keep safe.

Place your box somewhere like this and then ask the children to cover the box with logs, twigs and bark, and place a few leaves inside. They should put the majority of the twigs, leaves and grass they have collected just outside the doorway. Leave a tasty meal for your hedgehog, such as specially-made hedgehog food, or dog or cat food, near the entrance of the home so they feel welcome.

Further ideas for investigation

Create a large map of your wildlife area and put it on the classroom wall. Encourage the children to record what animals, plants and fungi they see living in the different areas throughout the year.

Can weeds help us?

This activity provides opportunities to observe and record living things, and helps children to understand plant reproduction and food chains.

> **Links to other activities:** The following activities work well in combination with this one as they all cover seeds, planting, growing and pollinators. You may wish to run these together as part of an after-school gardening club.
>
> - Seeds of time
> - Bioblitz investigation
> - Berry nice
> - Plants vs. pests
> - Bring in the bees

Materials

- Two patches or areas of flowering plants (with a minimum of six plants) – these will be your 'focal' plants.
    - These can be in pots, growbags or a vegetable patch.
    - Ensure these have fruits or seeds you can count easily.
    - These should ideally include edible plants, such as tomatoes, peppers, chillies, strawberries, raspberries, redcurrants, broad beans, peas or courgettes, but you could also use sweet peas, cowslips or dahlias.
- Weeding tools, e.g. small trowels or hand forks
- Small watering cans or similar

Optional:

- Wildflower identification sheets (which can be downloaded from a range of reliable organisations, such as Plantlife)
- Pollinator identification sheets (available from Buglife and the Natural History Museum)
- Thin recycled paper tape or similar
- Non-toxic waterproof paint

Activity

> **Teacher tip**
> The two patches of flowering 'focal' plants for this activity don't have to be uniform in shape or size, but they should have the same number of flowering plants (of the same species) within them, with one of them well-weeded and the other left weedy. One easy way of setting this activity up is to place the same number of potted plants (all the same type of plant) in two spots, one where there are no weeds around (e.g. on a patio or paved area) and one in a weedy grass area (ideally with flowering weeds). It is best if the two patches are at least ten metres apart, but you can still give the experiment a go with less space.

Pollinator predictions

Start the activity by asking the children to describe the two patches. What are the differences in the environments of the focal plants? Tell the children that the weedy patch has more plant biodiversity than the non-weedy patch. Ask them what insects might be living in both the patches – it's likely that there will be a greater diversity of insects in the weedy patch. How will this affect pollination of our potted plants? Tell the children they are going to set up an experiment to investigate how weeds affect the seed production of the focal plants.

Discuss what insects might visit and pollinate the flowering plants in the experiment (e.g. bees, flies, butterflies, beetles and even wasps). The introductory discussion in the 'Bring in the bees' activity can work well as a starting point for this activity too. The children might want to come up with hypotheses for what they think they will find when they compare their results of the number of insects visiting the flowers of the focal plants in each patch. They could also come up with other hypotheses, or predictions, such as if they think differences in insect visitors to the plants will mean a difference in the number of fruits the plants develop in the two patches.

Recording data

Ask the children to record the numbers of flying insects that visit the focal plants' flowers in each patch within a given time frame. Depending on the size of the group and your patches, you could create a pollinator-watch rota so that the children take it in turns to record flower visitors for a certain amount of time every day or week (around 20 minutes on a dry and not-too-windy day is ideal). Just ensure each patch is observed the same number of times and for the same amount of time during each pollinator-watch session.

As well as recording the numbers of flying insects visiting the flowers, you could encourage the children to try and record the types of visitor – you could use broad groups to avoid them having to look through lots of ID charts, e.g. bees, flies, butterflies and beetles. This will indicate the diversity of insects visiting the flowers of the focal plants. Hopefully there will be a difference in both the numbers of individual flower visits and the numbers of different types of insect flower visitors between the weedy and the non-weedy plant patches. Ecology studies like this do have lots of variables that can affect insect visitors, however – see the discussion section below.

The children can also apply their understanding of a fair test throughout this activity. For example, encourage them to measure the amount of water they give to the plants each day and to try to make sure both plant patches have a similar amount of shade. Get the children involved in taking out weeds that develop in between the focal plants in the non-weedy patch. For the weedy patch, you should also remove any weeds that get very large and significantly increase shading of the focal plant species. You could also spend one session recording the number of different plants that are growing alongside the focal plant species.

The next part of the investigation can start when some fruits or seed-pods start appearing on the plants in both patches. The children can collect the fruits as they form to record the number that way, or find some way of marking those they have already counted (e.g. with thin tape around the tops of the fruits, or waterproof non-toxic paint). This can continue until all the flowers in both patches have died away. Depending on the types of fruit or pod, the children could also measure the number of seeds from a sub-sample of the pods.

Discussion

Ask the children to look at their observation results and discuss if there are any differences in a) the number of flower visitors, b) the number of different types of flower visitor, and c) the number of fruits or seeds produced by the plants in the weedy patch vs. the non-weedy patch. The results of this experiment can vary. The hypothesis that flowering weeds attract more flower visitors to the focal plants (leading to more fruit production) does not always turn out to be the case. You might get more flower visitors in the weedy patch but record fewer fruits than in the non-weedy patch. These kinds of unexpected results are common in ecology because there are so many variables. You can talk to the children about the other factors that might affect the amount of successful pollination. For example, there might be more herbivorous insects in the weedy patch that eat the flowers before they can develop into fruits.

On the other hand, if the results show that there were more flower visits and more diversity of insects visiting the flowers *and* a higher number of fruits produced, the children can make some links between insect pollinators and the production of fruits and vegetables. You can also discuss how intensive farming aims to eliminate all weeds and pests, but perhaps this is not the best approach – we might be able to attract more pollinators if we let our orchards and crop fields get a bit weedy.

Further ideas for investigation

This activity could run over the course of a few months, with the children starting the activity by sowing seeds to create their flowering patches. Growing a tray or bed of plants from seed offers many opportunities to learn about the different parts of plants, and how and what they need to grow. 'Sunflower power' and 'Seeds of time' include examples of growing edible plants and using the seeds in particular. Further activities include the following.

- Once you have counted the number of fruits or pods from each patch, cut them open and encourage children to draw them.
- Collect and dry the seeds for future growing.
- Ask children to spot and name other 'pests' that eat the fruits, seeds or leaves in the patches, e.g. birds, slugs and snails.
- Encourage the children to draw labelled diagrams of bees and other pollinators, thinking about how they're adapted to visit flowers and collect nectar and pollen. (See 'Bring in the bees' for more on this.)

Plants vs. pests

What do we mean by a pest? What is a weed? Explore how human cultivation of food to feed our growing population means we've 'changed' nature. In this activity, the children can try out some more-natural (and slightly smelly) alternatives to using fertilisers and pesticides.

> **Links to other activities:** Other plant- and scent-based activities that you might like to run over a period of time alongside this one include 'What on earth?', 'Can weeds help us?' and 'Makes a lot of scents'.

Materials

Required:

- A flower-bed, vegetable patch or potted plants with established plants or crops (and ideally a few weeds)
- Two containers with lids (ideally small water butts or buckets with lids)
- Banana peelings
- Weeds
- Collected rainwater
- Small watering cans or similar
- Garlic
- A pestle and mortar
- A large jar with a lid
- Eco washing-up liquid
- Cheese cloth or similar
- A fine-meshed sieve
- A spray bottle

Optional:

- A funnel or similar

Activity

You can run these two activities at the same time and with the same plants. The best time of year to run them is in the spring when populations of pests and weeds have started to build up, so there will be plenty of examples to find and discuss.

Introducing natural fertilisers

Ask the children to look at the plants and see if they can point out which plants growing there are weeds, and which are ones that humans have put there for a reason (i.e. to look nice or to grow food). Lots of children won't recognise a weed from a cultivated plant or crop and that can be a great point to start a discussion about the word 'weed'. Weeds are plants that naturally start growing in an area where humans are trying to grow food such as vegetables, or ornamental plants like daffodils and roses. Humans have labelled these plants as weeds that need to be removed because they can make our crops grow less well. Farmers and gardeners sometimes use chemicals called weedkillers (or herbicides) to get rid of weeds to stop them affecting the growth of important crops like wheat and potatoes. In a smaller garden, you can just remove weeds with gardening tools.

Tell the children that these collected weeds can actually be turned into useful things called fertilisers. Fertilisers are added to the soil to help plants grow better and more quickly. They contain nutrients, which plants need alongside water and light energy to grow and develop. Chemical fertilisers can be helpful for growing enough food to feed us all, but adding lots of these nutrients to soils where crops grow in large areas can have very negative effects on nearby wildlife and their habitats. For example, the fertilisers can flow into rivers and cause lots of algae to grow. The algae use up the oxygen and block the sunlight, leading to the death of fish and other aquatic wildlife.

Making natural fertiliser – bananas to the rescue!

There are more-natural ways to add nutrients to the soil where plants are growing than giving them chemical fertilisers. Tell the children that they are going run an experiment to make two different types of natural fertiliser and see which one works best.

Put the collected weeds in one container and the banana peelings in the other. Pour in enough water that it just covers the weeds and peelings, and then put the lids on the containers. Leave for a minimum of two weeks and then uncover – and warn the children it is a bit smelly. Mix a small amount of each type of fertiliser with some water in separate labelled watering cans (about ten parts water to one part fertiliser), and then use this to water your plants. Split the bed or pots into two so one side receives the weed 'tea' and the other receives the banana 'tea'.

Encourage the children to take it in turns every day to water the plants with the fertiliser mixes and to record any differences in the numbers or sizes of flowers, fruits, leaves or vegetables. Introduce elements of a fair test into this activity from the outset. For example, ask the children to think about what factors other than the different fertilisers might affect plant growth (e.g. sunlight, water and the amount of fertiliser) and if they can find ways to keep these other factors the same between the two experimental groups. It is a good idea to add in a third 'control' test here, in which plants receive water only.

Bananas contain potassium, which can increase flower and fruit growth in many plants. Weeds store nutrients such as phosphorus and nitrogen from the soil in their leaves and roots, so the fertiliser made of weeds will give your plants a concentrated boost of these nutrients. You should see more flower and leaf growth in the plants given the fertilisers compared to those given only water. Different plant species will vary in their responses to the banana fertiliser vs. the weed fertiliser. Encourage the children to observe and record differences by counting the leaves and flowers and measuring plant height.

Introducing pests – garlic keeps the insect pests away!

Introduce the concept of a 'pest' in relation to growing crops and plants by encouraging the children to look for aphids or other easily recognisable insects on the plants. It would be worth having a look before the session in case your plants are pest-free – if that's the case, you might want to skip the initial pest-hunt and make the garlic spray to use at a later date or another location. In any case, you can still discuss plant pests and why humans try to control them.

Explain to the children that, when humans grow lots of the same plant in one spot, it attracts lots of insects that like to feed on this kind of plant. They can reproduce very quickly and cause lots of damage, reducing the amount of the plant we have left to eat or enjoy looking at.

Humans have tried to control these pests in various ways, including using chemical insect killers (insecticides). These chemicals can be harmful to other insects that are actually beneficial to our plants (e.g. pollinators), so it's important we try to avoid using these in our own gardens. Show the children the garlic and tell them that lots of insect pests are put off by the smell of garlic; they're not harmed by it but they want to avoid going near it. So we can make a natural insect-pest repellent with garlic, water and soap that we can spray on plants to protect them from getting munched on by hungry aphids, beetles and other pests.

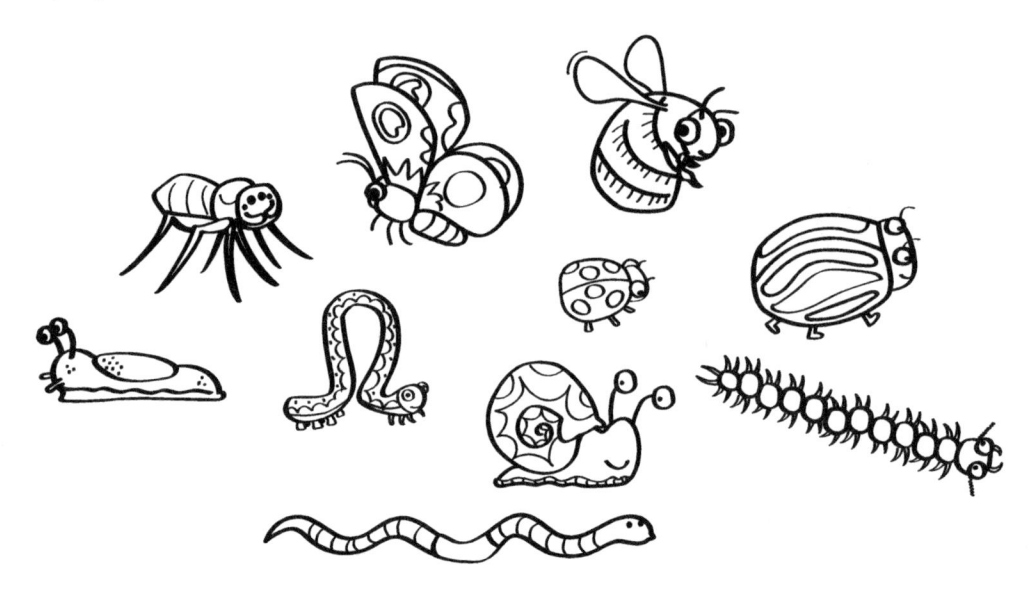

Making garlic pest repellent

To make the spray, break up the bulb of garlic and peel off the skins – this is a task children can share. Crush the garlic up in a pestle and mortar (which the children can take turns doing) and then put it into the jar, along with about a litre of water and two tablespoons of eco washing-up liquid. Explain that the soap will help the mixture stick to the plants and can also help with repelling insects. Put the lid on the jar and leave the mixture to steep for a few days.

Line the sieve with the cheesecloth, and then place it over the bowl. Pour the mixture into the sieve and squeeze the cheesecloth to remove as much of the liquid as possible. Transfer the mixture to the spray bottle (which might require a funnel). Now you're ready to test out the garlic spray. You could compare its effectiveness by spraying some infested plants and others with water alone. Store the mixture in the refrigerator and use within a week.

Further ideas for investigation

You could compare garlic pest spray with one containing alternative strong-smelling foods such as onions, chilli and cayenne pepper (although care is needed when handling these, so see the Safety note in 'Seed-sational' on page 82) and see which one keeps pests away the best. You could also extend this by learning about insect-plant interactions by encouraging the children to record all the minibeasts they see on a plant, working out if they are 'friend' or 'foe'.

You could also explain companion planting to the children, where growers plant flowering plants such as marigolds or nasturtiums alongside pest-prone crops like beans to attract insects away from our food crops. You could try this with your plants and see if placing these flowering plants reduces the numbers of pest insects on your vegetable crops.

The wonderful world of worms

Charm some worms by pretending to be rain and learn what they (and other soil-dwelling critters) do for soils and for human beings. It's best to do this activity on a dry day (or it can get a bit too mucky), but not during a drought as the worms will be too far underground and will take too long to burrow up.

> **Links to other activities:** 'Bioblitz investigation' and 'Reduce; reuse; recycle' both discuss biodiversity as well as the environmental advantages of worms. 'Tiny plastic everywhere' also covers how microplastics can be harmful to worms.

Materials

- A bare patch of soil
- Children's wellies or shoes that can get a bit mucky
- Hand lenses

Optional:

- Percussion instruments, e.g. drums, tambourines or maracas
- Small plant jars or similar, containing moist soil

Activity

Ask the children if they can name any living things that you can find in the soil. Hopefully they will give worms as an answer. Ask them if they can think about when they are most likely to see worms, i.e. in wet weather. Worms find it easier to move across the soil surface, find a mate and find new sources of food when it is wet, so when they hear the vibrations of rain from underground they start to burrow upwards. We can 'charm' worms to the surface by pretending to be rain.

Give each child a percussion instrument (optional) and show them the worm-charming area – a cleared area of soil works well. Ask them to walk around the area of soil (without stamping) and to clap or play their percussion instrument. To avoid collisions, it's a good idea to have half the children walking around on the soil and the other half on worm watch, so those who are walking and playing instruments can look where they're going.

Once the worms start appearing (hopefully after ten minutes or so), encourage the children to stop walking over the soil and to collect worms onto a plain surface like a bench or into their soil-filled containers. Make sure they collect only worms that are fully on the surface of the soil and they don't try to pull any out that are still half burrowed. Then the worm-watchers can swap with the other group and charm some more worms up to the surface.

Encourage the children to take a closer look at the worms and look at their bodies under hand lenses. Can they work out which end of a worm is the mouth end? Can they see different types of worms amongst the ones they have collected? There are 31 species of earthworm in the UK, so you might have a few represented among your charmed worms.

Ask the children to describe the worms' bodies. They might notice that they look like they're made up of little rings fused together. You can then tell them that an earthworm's body is made of about 100–150 segments or sections. Each segment or section has muscles, and bristles called setae. The setae help anchor and control the worm when it's moving through soil. Inside the muscular outer body of a worm is a digestive tube.

If there are any worms in those collected that have a white, orange-red or reddish-brown band in one section of their bodies, these are sexually mature worms. This band is called a clitellum and is the reproductive part of a worm. Although worms are hermaphrodites (both male and female), they still need to mate with another worm to reproduce. Hatchlings (baby worms) develop in cocoons.

> **Teacher tip**
>
> Ensure you return the collected worms to the soil after the worm-charming and discussion (or after the wormery activity in 'Further ideas for investigation').

Why do we need worms?

Ask the children if they can think of what worms do in the soil and how worms help us. Some of them might know that they help gardeners and provide food for birds. They might be less likely to know these fun worm facts:

- Worms eat lots of different things that are found in the soil, including dead plants, fallen leaves, fungi, bacteria and even dead animals. They can eat the equivalent of their own body weight every day.
- When they eat, worms break down and recycle all these things in the soil, which helps naturally fertilise the earth and ensure it is packed with the nutrients essential for plants to grow. Without worms, our soil wouldn't be as good at growing all the delicious fruits and vegetables we eat.
- Worm casts (the little mounds you sometimes see on the surface of the soil) contain nutrients called nitrogen and phosphorus, and lots of beneficial bacteria that help plants thrive.
- Worms loosen, mix and oxygenate the soil as they burrow channels through it.
- They improve soil's structure, leaving space for water to be drained away from the surface and stored in the soil.
- Worms' wriggling and burrowing movements help distribute beneficial bacteria and other useful microorganisms more evenly in the soil.
- Worms are very important in the food chain. They provide a crucial protein-rich source of food for other species like birds, hedgehogs and frogs.

In summary, without soil organisms like worms, which eat living and dead animal and plant material and turn it into nutrients, no plants could grow.

Further ideas for investigation

If you have lots of space for the worm-charming activity, you could make it competitive by dividing up the area of soil into a grid and seeing how many worms each group can charm.

Set up a mini wormery by adding layers of leaf litter, sand and soil to some large jars. You can add the worms you've charmed up from the soil and see what happens to the layers as they burrow through them.

The children could also investigate some of the other living things found in soil. There are up to 1.5 kg of living organisms living beneath one square metre of healthy soil, including threadworms, earthworms, springtails, mites, insect larvae, protists, bacteria, fungi and many more. Some won't be visible to the naked eye but having a look through collected soil can be a great way to increase the children's awareness of the biodiversity beneath our feet.

Rain savers

Use a rainy day to encourage the children to think about the importance of water through a rainwater-harvesting challenge.

> **Links to other activities:** 'Water day' is another activity involving how both we and plants rely on water and 'Changing colours' goes into more detail about pH.

Materials

- Containers of various sizes, such as jars, bottles, tin cans and bowls (which you can ask the children to collect over the summer holidays, ahead of rainy days in the autumn term)
- Permanent markers
- Stones or pebbles (to weigh down lighter containers)
- A water butt
- Measuring jugs
- Potted plants: ericaceous (acid-loving) plants like azaleas, camellia or blueberry plants if possible, as these are likely to give the most observable differences

Activity

Rainwater harvesting was carried out by everyone before we had mains water supply. Today we pay little attention to the amount of water we use every day, and the amount that is wasted. As climate change increasingly affects rainfall patterns, hosepipe bans are frequent in many parts of the UK. That means collecting water during the wetter days and months, and storing it for watering plants on dryer days and in periods of drought, is becoming more and more important.

Harvesting rainwater

Explain that the children are having a rainwater-harvesting challenge. Ask the children to choose a container each, and a spot outside where they think they will collect the most rainwater. Each child can label their container with their name using a permanent marker (on the bottom if possible, as this spot will stay the driest).

Encourage them to try and find a position for their rain harvester where rain is not doing an important job like watering plants or grass (but how feasible this is will be dependent on your outdoor space). Ask children who chose lighter containers like plastic yoghurt pots to weigh these down with stones or similar in the bottom.

Leave the containers to collect rain for a day or two and then collect them and start to measure the amount of water each has collected using a measuring jug. You could create a leader board to keep a record of whose container has collected the most rain.

After each container's water has been measured, transfer it to a water butt with a lid, as it needs to be stored well to stop it going stagnant. After this activity, the water butt can be used to collect water as in an ordinary garden and this can then be used for lots of watering and water-based activities throughout the year.

Watering experiment

Use the collected rainwater for a watering experiment. For this, you need 6–8 potted plants (e.g. azaleas), which can be kept in a glasshouse or on a windowsill. Ask the children to water the plants with a small amount of either rainwater or tap water each day. They should agree on the amount the plants will receive on a daily basis, and use separate labelled measuring jugs for the two types of water to ensure a fair test. (The plants need to be kept indoors or sheltered so that those being watered with tap water don't accidentally get some rainwater too, when it rains).

Hopefully the children will be able to observe some differences in the plants watered with rainwater and those watered with tap water. They might look more healthy and lush, and have more leaves. This is because rainwater is slightly more acidic than tap water and doesn't contain chlorine, fluorine, minerals and coagulants, which are all in treated tap water. These minerals raise the pH of the water and can affect the nutrient availability for plants. This is particularly important for ericaceous (acid-loving) plants. See 'Changing colours' for more about the pH scale.

Further ideas for investigation

You could use litmus paper or some other indicator to test the pH of rainwater vs. tap water. Is there an observable difference or is a more-sensitive test (such as with Universal pH indicator paper) needed?

What else could we use rainwater for, as well as watering plants? Ask the children to come up with ideas for using collected rainwater in their everyday lives to help reduce the water we consume in our homes, schools and gardens (e.g. for painting or art sessions, in the school kitchen for washing vegetables, and for cleaning and mopping).

Ice to see you

This activity helps the children understand how ice behaves, what this means for the ice currently on our planet, and the impact of this as the climate changes. This is perfect for a wintery or snowy day, but can also be carried out at any time of year using ice cubes.

> **Links to other activities:** 'The big freeze' also uses ice and 'Circle of influence' covers discussions about climate change and the environment.

Materials

Required:

- A deep tray or cake tin (without removable bottom), or a plant-free area of soil and an empty compost bag
- Collected rainwater
- Soil, compost or a small container (to use as land in your demonstration)
- Snow or ice cubes
- A twig or ruler

Optional:

- A trowel or small spade
- A marker pen
- Cold water
- Hot or warm water (not boiling)
- Natural food colouring

Activity

Ask the children what they know about ice and snow: how does it feel, what does it look like and where do you find it? Explain that ice is the solid form of water, and snow is like rain but it occurs when the water vapour in the atmosphere falls as ice crystals instead of as water.

Do the children know where the Arctic and Antarctic are, and that penguins are found in the Antarctic and polar bears in the Arctic? Next time they watch a cartoon with a penguin and polar bear duo, they will know that in real life those two would never have met.

What is ice like in water?

> **Safety note**
>
> This activity might be best as a class demonstration because of the materials needed, with individual children volunteering to demonstrate.

Find out what the children think about the icebergs and ice sheets in the Arctic and Antarctic. Does the ice go all the way down into the water? Explain that the ice can be quite deep in some places, but the ice is actually floating on the water.

Fill the deep tray or cake tin with water halfway, or dig a small space in a plant-free area of soil and use an empty compost bag as a liner (almost as if you're making a pond) and fill this halfway up with water. Help the children add a small mound of moistened soil or compost (or a small upturned jar) to represent land at one end.

Dip a ruler or twig into the water to note the level of the water. The children may wish to use a marker pen to mark a line on the twig, or you can use your nails to scratch into it. Ask the children to pop an ice cube or a snowball into the water. What happens to the water level? What happens as the ice melts?

Pop some ice cubes or snow onto the 'land' that the children have created. What does it look like? The snow on the land should look like the snow in the water. In real life, it's sometimes hard to tell if there's land underneath large bodies of ice, but around the world we have lots of ice on land in glaciers and mountain ranges. What do the children think will happen if the ice on land melts?

Leave this set up for the ice to melt on the land too. If it's a particularly cold day, you might want to set this up indoors so the melting will be quicker.

What the children will see

When ice is added to the water, the water level should rise; the water will come up higher than the marked point on the twig or ruler. However, as the ice melts the water level will remain the same. This means that, when the ice in the Arctic or Antarctic that floats on the water begins to melt, the sea levels won't rise. However, as the ice on the 'land' melts, it will drain into the rest of the water and will cause the water levels to rise further up the twig or ruler.

Ask the children what they think rising sea levels will mean, such as what happens to habitats when the ice begins to melt. If there's no ice, what would happen to the animals that live on the ice in the Arctic and Antarctic?

Explain that, as the global temperature rises, the ice melts, but it is the melting of ice on land that will cause sea levels to rise the most. This will lead to flooding and the coasts will start to erode or wear away (with habitable land space shrinking).

Further ideas for investigation

You can demonstrate the temperature change of water to the children by pouring some cold water into a glass and adding some warm water dyed with food colouring gently on the top. The coloured warm water will float on top of the cold water. Ask the children what they understand by this. Why does the warm water float?

Explain that there is another reason why the sea levels can rise as the planet warms up. As the sea water becomes warmer, it will start to expand. In the same way that hot air rises because it has expanded and become less dense, warm water becomes less dense too. Warmer water takes up much more space and will cause sea levels to rise.

What do the children think about climate change and global warming? Encourage a discussion with the children about what it will mean for biodiversity on land and in water as the planet warms. Habitats will be lost and many creatures cannot survive in warmer waters and climates.

Reassure the children that all is not lost. Scientists and governments around the world are working together to help reduce global temperatures by reducing our greenhouse-gas emissions. They are also researching new technologies to help do this, such as electric vehicles, renewable energies like solar and wind power, and ways to capture and store carbon so it doesn't reach the atmosphere.

Tiny plastic everywhere

This activity demonstrates how microplastics quickly spread in an environment. Microplastics are extremely small pieces of plastic debris in the environment resulting from the disposal and breakdown of consumer products and industrial waste.

> **Links to other activities:** 'Natural manufacturing', 'Picking straws' and 'Wear on earth' look at creatively using natural alternatives to plastic. 'Reduce; reuse; recycle' and 'Circle of influence' also focus on similar environmental issues.

Materials and equipment

Required:

- Fizzy drink cans
- Clothing items made of synthetic fibres, e.g. fleece tops and pairs of leggings
- A washing-up sponge
- Sun cream
- Rulers
- Dead leaves
- Trays
- Water in a watering can (ideally rainwater) or a hosepipe with a spray fitting
- A bare patch of soil or similar
- A trowel or small spade

Optional

- One-hole hole punches (ideally one per child)

Activity

What are microplastics?

Start by passing around the plastic waste items and discuss what could happen to them after they're thrown away. Some can be recycled and turned into other things but lots of plastic items can end up polluting our environment. They can be harmful to wildlife as big pieces of plastic but they can also cause damage once they've started to break up into small pieces. They become microplastics: very tiny pieces of plastic that spread everywhere via rivers and seas, and can be swallowed by animals and even humans. For example, tyres on cars lose tiny bits of plastic rubber every time the car is driven. These end up being washed into rivers by the rain.

Ask the children if they have heard about microplastics on the news or anywhere else. Tell them that microplastics are plastic pieces that measure less than five millimetres across. Pass the rulers around and encourage the children to see what five millimetres looks like. Some are even smaller, so small you can't see them.

Explain that, as well as plastic rubbish and tyres, there are other more-surprising things that cause microplastic pollution. For example, metal fizzy drink cans (hold up the can) often have a plastic coating on them. Clothes made of synthetic fibres (hold up the clothing) shed tiny bits of plastic every time they are washed. Every time you wash up with a washing-up sponge (hold up sponge), tiny pieces of plastic go down the plugholes and into our water systems. And some products like sunscreen (hold up the sunscreen) have teeny tiny ball-shaped microplastics called microbeads added to them.

These can all get washed into our rivers and water systems and then end up in our food and atmosphere. Scientists are doing lots of studies about the effects of microplastics on the health of humans and other living things. Some of their experiments have shown that these tiny pieces of plastic can damage the cells that make up animals and other living things. (Cells are the tiny building blocks of all living things.) More studies are needed to understand if this could lead to illnesses or other problems in humans or other animals.

Demonstrating the spread of microplastics in the environment

Ask the children to collect up some dead leaves from the floor and place them on the trays (trying to go to a sheltered spot if it is a windy day). Explain that we are going to imagine the leaves are bits of plastic waste and use the hole punches to create our own microplastics. Demonstrate this and then give the children ten minutes or so to hole-punch lots of leaves onto their trays. You could ask them to tear the leaves into tiny pieces if hole punches aren't available.

Explain that now we are going to watch where the bits of leaves, our pretend microplastics, go on a patch of soil. 'Wash' them off the trays using a watering can (or hose on a low-pressure spray setting) to mimic the effect of rain on the spread of microplastics in an environment. Each group can bring up their tray of leaf pieces and watch as they are washed off the tray onto the soil. You can then add more water and even dig a trench and wash them into it to show how microplastics can flow into other areas in an environment.

This activity can lead into a wider discussion about what effects microplastic pollution might have on living things in different environments. We often hear about the negative effects of plastic pollution in our oceans, but studies have also shown that around a third of all plastic waste ends up in soils and rivers. These same studies showed harmful effects on animals that live in these habitats, like worms.

Further ideas for investigation

As a follow-up class or group project, the children could invent alternatives for some everyday plastic items, coming up with ideas for reducing plastic waste and pollution. This links well to learning about the properties of different materials, and can help the children think about the impact of human behaviour (both positive and negative) on environments.

Picking straws

Learn about the different parts of plants and how this could be the answer to our plastics crisis.

Links to other activities: Understanding about plant stems also occurs in 'Weave got strength' and 'The hole illusion'. 'Guess who?' and 'Tiny plastic everywhere' involve observation on a small scale, with the latter also discussing plastics in our environment.

Materials

Required:

- A variety of plant stalks, such as dandelions, courgettes, alliums, dahlias, salsify or even bamboo

Optional:

- Scissors or secateurs
- Hand lenses or a small digital microscope (linked to a screen)
- Celery stalks

Activity

Start by asking the children the last time they had a drink through a straw. Was it a plastic straw? Find out what they think about plastic straws and the environment. They may have seen wildlife television programmes about the harm plastic causes to the marine environment. Thanks to such programmes and increasing awareness of the issues, it's now more common to be given paper straws at restaurants and cafés in the UK, and more difficult to buy disposable plastic straws.

Finding a straw

Ask the children: which part of the plant is the stalk? Explain that it is the main stem that supports the flowers, leaves and fruit. Many plants that self-seed in gardens and fields, such as dandelions, can have hollow stalks. The children can have a go at exploring plants to see if they can find anything with a hollow stalk. Have a few examples on hand (as listed above) in case they don't find any. Most grasses and flowers of the allium family (e.g. leeks, garlic and chives) have hollow stalks. Courgette stems might be a little prickly, so do warn the children. You may need to help them cut the stalks.

Ask the children to look closely at the stalks. What can they see around the edges? They could use hand lenses or a digital microscope to study their stalks. Can they see through the stalks? Do the children think these could be used as natural alternatives to drinking straws? (Maybe not, if they're prickly!) If possible, show the children a dried allium stem, as these are often used as homegrown straws.

What the children will see

Explain that hollow-stemmed plants are lighter, so can sway more easily in the wind without breaking. However, if the children observe the cross-section of the stalk once cut, they'll notice many dots. These are the 'straws' inside the plant. Explain that all plants need to transport water and food (sugars and other nutrients) through lots of tubes. Water travels through xylem tubes and food through phloem tubes.

Further ideas for investigation

Ask the children in groups or pairs whether they can actually pour water through their found straws. This may be a little difficult for very thin tube stalks. In countries where papayas grow, the children often use the hollow stalks to create water-pipe systems to play with and see how far the water will travel.

The children can also try looking at stalks of celery and pulling the tubes (xylem and phloem) out from the sides. These are very thin strands, and can be peeled out from just under the skin of the celery. The cross-section of the celery will then have holes where the tubes once were.

Can the children think of other uses of the plants they see around them? Brambles and roses have spiky thorns on their stalks, which can be cut and used as barriers to deter pests such as slugs from eating vegetables on allotments. Plant seeds have led to inventions too: Velcro® was invented by electrical engineer George de Mestral after his dog got covered in burrs (hooked seeds) that stuck to his dog's fur. This may have been the seeds' way of getting dispersed, but gave de Mestral an idea for a new type of strong fastening.

Natural manufacturing

Many children's toys contain materials such as plastics, which break down into smaller plastic pieces (or microplastics) and cause damage in the environment. This activity will show the children an environmentally friendly process to manufacture a toy using natural materials, which will decompose easily once thrown away.

> **Links to other activities:** 'Wear on earth' and 'Weave got strength' both involve creating items out of natural materials. The 'Tiny plastic everywhere' activity covers similar environmental topics, such as microplastics and biodegradation.

Materials

Required:

- A variety of natural items, such as twigs, bark, leaves, grasses, feathers, flowers, seeds, pinecones, acorns, conkers and pebbles
- Hole punches
- Scissors

Optional:

- Thick paste made from flour and water (in jar lids or bowls)
- Paintbrushes

Activity

Ask the children about their favourite toys now or when they were younger, and whether anyone still has theirs. If not, where are they? What materials are most toys made of? Explain that many toys are made of or contain plastics. Objects made from mixtures of plastics often cannot be recycled and will end up in landfill, where they slowly break down into tiny pieces of plastic that can end up damaging our land and ocean wildlife. These microplastics can even end up in our food and drinking water. (See 'Tiny plastic everywhere' for more on microplastics.)

Making a simple figurine

Give the children ten minutes to find some items outdoors to make a small toy or puppet. You don't need to give too many instructions at this point, but maybe a little guidance as to what they need to think about in terms of building their toy. For example, wrapping twigs with leaves and tying them together with long grasses can help form body shapes, while flowers (or even pressed flowers) can make great faces, hands and feet. Hole punches and scissors can be used to cut out shapes (such as eye holes) from leaves, petals and feathers.

If they wish to make an environmentally friendly glue, mixing some flour and water into a thick paste and applying it with paintbrushes can help the children see that their toys can be decorated beautifully and be fully compostable too. They might make a doll, bear or an alien... whatever their imaginations allow.

Why natural materials?

Explain that by using materials available in nature we are not manufacturing more plastic, which leads to plastic waste and damage to the environment. Natural materials such as grasses, twigs, bark and so on will break down naturally (or decompose) in the environment. Decomposition is caused by microorganisms including bacteria and fungi, and this process adds nutrients back into the soil. This means, when a toy made from natural materials is thrown away, it will biodegrade and its nutrients returned to the soil to help something new to grow.

Further ideas for investigation

What have the children understood about the different materials they're using? Which natural objects were best suited for constructing their toys and why? Which ones were strong, waterproof and easy to work with? Why stop at figurines? Can the children create natural moveable robots, cars and other vehicle toys?

You could add an entrepreneurial side to this activity to create cross-curricular links. If the children had to market their toys to other children, what posters would they create to encourage more young people to choose natural materials (in art)? How could they use persuasive writing to draft adverts or practise public speaking (in English)? How can they add adaptations to make their toys more enticing to play with, like moveable parts, outfits and accessories (in design and technology)? If the children had to sell these toys, how much would they sell them for (in maths)? Discuss how to decide the value of the toys, given that they may start to decompose and the materials were given to us by nature.

Wear on Earth

Learn about natural materials and how to create fashionable, sustainable accessories. This gives young people an opportunity to think about our world of fast fashion and its impact on our environment.

> **Links to other activities:** 'Weave got strength', 'Natural manufacturing', and 'Circle of influence' are all activities around using found and natural materials for combining environmental and entrepreneurial learning.

Materials

Required:

- A variety of natural items, such as leaves, twigs, bark, flowers, grasses, pinecones, conkers, pebbles and stalks

Optional:

- Scissors

Activity

Ask the children what they think about fashion. Is it important for them to wear fashionable items? What do they do with clothes and accessories that are no-longer fashionable in their eyes, that they don't like any more or that they have grown out of?

Explain that waste is a huge problem in the fashion industry. Very little is recycled, donated or reused. Most of it is thrown into landfill or burned, and, when they're made from synthetic, plastic-based materials such as polyester, they can take around 200 years to decompose.

Why don't we look towards nature? Natural materials such as cotton, linen and bamboo are all made from plants. Every industry has its issues (for example, the amount of water that goes into creating one cotton shirt is the same amount of water a person can drink over two and a half years). However, the more natural a fabric is, the more likely it can decompose back into nutrients in the environment rather than causing damage. There are recycled fabrics, such as fleece made from recycled plastic bottles, but both washing them and throwing them away result in microplastics polluting the environment again.

Creating a natural fashion line

The children can work in pairs or groups. Ask them to spend some time finding a variety of items outdoors that they'd like to 'fashion' into some natural wearables.

See if the children notice how their own clothes are made. Can they see how the material is stitched together? Can they see the warp and weft threads woven in any of their clothes? Explain that the warp goes up and down and weft goes left to right. (You can remember this because weft rhymes with left.)

The children could weave or plait grasses, make daisy chains or tie flower stalks together to make bracelets, bangles, belts, headbands and hair accessories (as in the illustration below). They could use grasses and pinecones or flowers to create necklaces with pendants, rings and earrings. Ask them to create a few items to wear. Depending on the season, they will have access to a variety of coloured blossoms, leaves and seeds.

What the children will see

Ask the children what they each discovered when they made their new fashionable item. Was their accessory strong enough to wear? Plaited grasses may be stronger than, say, a daisy chain.

Grasses can be woven the same way as threads are to create a fabric. In many countries around the world, grasses, long leaves and stems are woven to make hats, belts, baskets and mats. Ask the children if they can think of other examples they may have seen or heard about.

Environmental outdoor fashion show

In their pairs or groups, the children can take it in turns to show off their new fashion line to the rest of the group and explain in a few sentences what they created. How much would their items cost if they were sold to others? Nature may be giving material to us for free, but is it really free? The time taken for a tree to grow, the water, the energy from the Sun... should we put a price on these? What about if someone has taken time to water the plants too?

Ask the children what would happen if they now threw their fashionable items away. Where would the waste all go? Explain that, as it is all completely natural, it would break down naturally (or decompose) and end up as nutrients back in the earth. See 'Natural manufacturing' for more on the benefits of using natural materials.

Further ideas for investigation

Explain that it's not just the fashion industry causing so much waste to the environment, but also the food industry. Ask the children to think about the last time they had a takeaway or bought food from a supermarket. What was the packaging like?

You could demonstrate how, in some South-Asian cultures, disposable plates are made by taking leaves and using tiny twigs or pieces of dried grasses or bark to sew them together. Even in restaurants, people may eat on large banana leaves, or food can be taken away wrapped in these. In South America, foods like tamales are steamed in corn husks too. Ask the children what they think happens to these forms of packaging when they are thrown away. In contrast, what happens to plastic packaging?

What was here before us?

This structured activity can support learning about local environments and habitats, and broaden the children's contextual understanding of the human impact on nature and biodiversity.

> **Links to other activities:** The following activities also help the children think about placing themselves in the wider natural world: 'Bioblitz investigation', 'You're the lichen to my moss' and 'Circle of influence'.

Materials

Required:

- Access to the internet and research materials
- Exercise books and pencils (for recording their questions and research)

Optional:

- Tape measures (ideally 5–10 m retractable tape measures)
- Art materials, including collected natural objects

Activity

This activity works best as a series of sessions with the option of giving the children homework or self-led group research time. An alternative approach to the research phase of the activity is suggested for very young children. The structure of the activity is loosely based on Simon Beames's Outdoor Journeys model (2010).

> **Teacher tip**
>
> Before you start this activity, find out some facts about your site, including the age of the school building. Most schools will have records about this on site or in their digital archives. You can also ask your local history society or similar for this information and other fun facts for the children to use as starting-off points to make further investigations.

Questioning

Ask the children to look at the school buildings (or your home, if home-schooling) and to think about what might have been there before they were built. You can give them basic facts like the age of the building, etc. Tell the children that, when humans first lived in the UK thousands of years ago, there were no buildings or roads. In fact, most of the country was covered with woodland and grassland. There weren't even any farmers – early humans were hunter-gatherers, who ate wild plants and caught animals to eat as meat.

Ask the children to go on a 20-minute 'journey' around the site and to look at the plants and trees, and think about questions they would like to ask about what living things they see. Ask them to consider how they got here and what was here before us.

If there are large trees on site, some children might want to try and find out if they have been there longer than the buildings. You can use the girth of a tree to estimate its age to help the children answer this question. Use the tape measure to measure around the tree's trunk at about one metre from the ground. Then divide the measurement (in centimetres) by 2.5 cm to get an estimate of the tree's age. (See 'Sum it up' for more detail on estimating the ages of trees.)

Other children might look at a sports pitch or football field and come up with questions about what plants would have been there before the grass or artificial flooring. Even small cracks in the pavement and walls, or the surface of old fences, can provide habitat for some plants and lichen species.

It works well for the children to work in pairs to go around and come up with a few questions. Examples you could give at the beginning might include:

- Were there more trees here before the buildings?
- Were crops grown here before the roads and buildings?
- What habitats were removed in order to build here?
- Would those plants have been here before humans?
- What kinds of animals live on the site, and would there have been different animals living here before humans?
- What kinds of animals might have been here that are now extinct?
- How has this site changed over the last hundred, thousand or ten thousand years?

Spend ten minutes at the end of the session asking the children to share the questions they have devised with the rest of the group. Ask each pair to pick a question from their list that they would like to try and answer.

Independent research

Give each pair time to find out some answers to their chosen question. They can work on this during a supervised session or as homework. Explain that they will be asked to share what they find out with the rest of the group in a presentation, and that they can use visual aids such as photos or their own artwork (ideally created using natural materials), or even perform re-enactments or dramatic interpretations. Plan the presentation session to take place outdoors, challenging the children to create something that doesn't require electricity or the internet.

They could, of course, use the internet and books to find out facts to answer their chosen questions, but encourage them also to think about how local museums or experts could help. Find out if your area has a local history society as they might have photos of the school site and local vicinity that will help them answer some of the children's questions. The children might want to go on additional visits around the site to look for more clues and information, maybe taking photos to include in their presentations.

For younger age groups, you could ask them to work on a piece of art to share with the group, based on what living things they saw on their journey around the site.

Sharing the findings

Hold a presentation session with enough time for each pair to present their question, how they researched the answer and what facts and answers they found out. Hold the session outdoors and move around the site where possible, to hear about the natural history of particular spots where the children based their questions.

As more of the pairs present their findings, you can make links between related questions and answers and discuss the different roles of plants and animals in the ecosystem. For example, trees and plants produce oxygen via photosynthesis, which allows animals (including humans) to breathe. Since humans started polluting the Earth's atmosphere by burning fossil fuels, plants and trees have also protected us from air pollution. They efficiently remove harmful pollutants such as carbon dioxide, nitrogen dioxide and sulphur dioxide. If any of the children have found out that the site was previously farmed for crops, you could also discuss monocultures and consider how the diversity of plants on site might have in fact increased since that time (e.g. due to more grassy or planted areas).

Discussions will vary depending on the range of questions asked and answered. Some children might be inspired to ask follow-up questions and find out more about what was here before us. Use the presentation material to create a timeline of the landscape of the site through the ages.

Further ideas for investigation

Follow this activity by considering how easy it would be to replace the wildlife and biodiversity that once was on your school site. Speak to your local Wildlife Trust about which species of wild plants, insects, birds and mammals are native to your region. Some might still be found there, using gardens and small urban green spaces as habitats, whereas others will be confined to specially managed nature reserves, or even not exist anywhere in the region or country any more. Can your group do anything to bring back any of the species that are now low in number or missing from our contemporary green spaces? See the Wildlife Trusts website for more ideas about rewilding your site.

Audio trails

This activity can help the children capture the sounds of the wildlife around them, learn to communicate like a scientist and share what they've learned with wider audiences through audio.

> **Links to other activities:** Other sound-based activities that work well alongside this one are 'Sound it out' and 'Music to my ears'. 'Circle of influence' also explores how we can use creative communication to spread important messages about the environment.

Materials

- Audio recording equipment, e.g. a mobile phone or tablet

Activity

Explain that conservation scientists who need to record wildlife sounds use audio technology, which can help work out where various species are located without actually having to see them.

Communicating their findings and area of research is a skill all scientists need, but they don't always do it through writing papers. Some may use television and video, while others might use audio forms like podcasts. Often the best way to communicate and reach wider audiences is through storytelling. In this activity, the children create an audio recording to share their findings from the great outdoors with others.

Starter: Recording and listening

Revisit how sound works from the 'Sound it out' activity. Ask the children to take it in turns to record some wildlife sounds, or whatever sounds they can find in their environment, working in pairs or small groups. If you have limited recording equipment, the groups not recording can be investigating the outdoor space to develop an audio trail as described below.

When everyone has created their recordings, play everything back to the group, pausing in between to find out what sounds everyone recognised. Were there any noises from wildlife, such as birdsong, leaves rustling or bees buzzing? How many sounds were made by humans, like children laughing, roadworks, traffic sounds or aeroplanes? Ask the children what they think about how noisy our environment is. What was their favourite sound?

Audio trails

In groups, ask the children to create audio trails around your outdoor area to take listeners on a journey around the space, incorporating sounds in the local environment. For example, the children could start at the school gate and explain that listeners need to walk so many steps towards a particular landmark (one that won't change) such as a tree or fence. Tell the children to give their listeners instructions, e.g. 'Stand here for one minute, and look to your left to see ...' and so on, encouraging their audience to notice things in the environment that they may usually overlook. This can also be in the form of a story or poem. Help the children to record their audio trails, each one lasting approximately 5–7 minutes.

The groups can then take it in turns to follow each other's trails and share what they learned. Explain to the children that museums, galleries, heritage sites and public gardens use this kind of audio tour to help tourists learn about their venues, and these can also be translated into many different languages. What kinds of fact or creative storytelling did the children add to their audio trails to keep their listeners' attention?

What the children will see

The children may notice more human noises than wildlife, especially depending on where you're running the activity. Ask them what they think this means in terms of local biodiversity. For example, more traffic noises means that land has been cleared to create roads for our vehicles. Where does wildlife go when this happens? Explain that this is what we mean by habitat loss.

Have the children heard of sound pollution? What do they think this means? Explain that, in the same way we have waste pollution on land and in our waterways harming nature, the levels of noise created by our vehicles and industries mean that wildlife can't communicate effectively with each other any more. They can't hear their mates' or babies' calls, or warnings of approaching predators. Scientists have found that traffic noise pollution reduces the amount of time birds will spend foraging for food, which can affect how healthy they are and how many babies they have (BBC News, 2021).

Further ideas for investigation

Ask the children about recording their performances in audio form. How would they describe everything that is happening so that a listener can 'see' what is happening? This can help the children to understand and empathise with those who have visual impairments, and how our other senses can support learning.

Children can also use performance storytelling to communicate everything that they've learned about nature and the environment. For example, they can enact the process of metamorphosis by acting as caterpillars turning into butterflies. Visualising performances like this in outdoor spaces can help consolidate learning and retain memories.

Circle of influence

Children all over the world want to know more about how they can help the environment in the fight against climate change. This activity can show them that they *do* have the power to influence the adults in their lives and can help bring about real change.

> **Links to other activities:** Other activities that cover environmental messaging and further useful information include 'Tiny plastic everywhere' and 'Reduce; reuse; recycle'.

Materials

Required:

- A variety of natural materials and items found outdoors
- Gloves (heavy duty or rubber if possible) or litter pickers for children
- Buckets or tote bags
- Access to water

Optional:

- Exercise books and pencils (for taking notes and researching)
- Arts and crafts materials (e.g. paint, string and containers)

Activity

With everything in the media causing alarm about climate change, it can be a pretty worrying time for many young people, especially as they may feel they can't change anything. But they *can* communicate through various methods (such as presentations, artwork and performances) and make adults in the community sit up and think, and even do something to affect change. By giving the children useful information and encouragement, we can support them to become active members of communities who make better decisions going forward, building a healthier environment for all.

Communicating messages further

Explain what 'circle of influence' means to the children: that individuals do have power and each one of us can have an impact, but it is all in how we creatively communicate the issues and influence others (who in turn influence even more people) to take action too. It's like a ripple effect in the water.

Taking the issue of littering and plastic pollution, tell the children of an example from the Galápagos Islands. Many island residents and visitors have no idea how much damage plastic is doing to the wildlife around the world: one million sea birds die from choking on plastic found in our oceans every year.

As part of the local organisation Grupo Eco Cultural Organizado (GECO), children collected plastic lids from fizzy drink bottles during their beach cleans and from urban areas, and used this collected plastic to create mini dolls. Those who made these dolls felt the need to stop using single-use plastics and wanted to encourage others to do the same (Guerrero and Klingman, 2018).

Children would carry their little dolls around, prompting conversations with family members and motivating the local community to think more about the plastic problem and how to change their behaviours (such as using reusable bags for shopping) in order to become part of the solution. Explain to children that influencing is not all about social media: we can have community-based social influence too.

Finding materials

Find out what your group thinks of this real-life example. Give the children a challenge: take them out on a litter-picking session to collect plastic waste (such as drinks bottles, lids, sweet wrappers, crisp packets and cartons) – you may wish to go to a local area you know is in need of some care. Once enough material has been collected, the items can be cleaned by being placed into a bucket of water and swirled around, and then left out to dry.

> **Safety note**
>
> Ask the children to wear gloves or use litter-pickers. You will need to supervise litter-picking in non-school areas in case of sharp objects and toxic materials.

Creating the installation

Find out what the children wish to create. Would it be more small characters like in the Galápagos example, and where would they display these? Could they create mini collages with natural materials and found plastic? Or perhaps use the pieces to create a large art installation of an endangered animal, which could be placed on display in the school reception, a local shopping centre or community area? The local mayor, councillors and community can be invited to an event to learn more about the issues of plastic pollution from the children, and be encouraged to make time-based pledges about how they intend to make a difference.

Further ideas for investigation

Start off by asking the children what they think about climate change, or any other environmental issues they have heard of and care about. Perhaps it's deforestation, sewage and pollutants in our rivers and air, the use of fossil fuels, loss of habitats and biodiversity, food waste, pollution from fast fashion, or something else.

Ask the children to think about their own strengths and talents, and how they would like to communicate creatively the issue closest to their hearts. Promoting these issues within the local community and offering people easy ways to take action (such as writing to the local council, signing petitions or reducing waste) can have a real impact, and offers hope for our citizens of tomorrow.

Bibliography

Beames, S. (2010). 'Outdoor Journeys'. Pathways: The Ontario Journal of Outdoor Education, 22 (Autumn), 4-5. See https://www.coeo.org/wp-content/uploads/pdfs/Digital_Pathways/Pathways_22_1.pdf

British Science Association (n.d.). CREST Awards. Available at: https://www.crestawards.org/ [Accessed 10.09.2024]

Buglife (n.d.). Bug Identification Tips. Available at: https://www.buglife.org.uk/bugs/bug-identification-tips/

Field Studies Council (n.d.). Wildlife guides and gifts. Available at: https://www.field-studies-council.org/shop/

Galapagos Conservation Trust (n.d.). Plastic-free Galapagos – Updates from our project partner Grupo Eco Cultural Organizado (GECO). Available at: https://galapagosconservation.org.uk/grupo-eco-cultural-organizado/

Gill, Victoria. (2021). 'Traffic noise impairs songbirds' abilities'. *BBC News*. Available at: https://www.bbc.com/news/science-environment-55910424

Guerrero Vela, J. and Klingman DeFever, A. (2018). Women Inspiring Change: Leadership for a Plastic-Free Culture in San Cristóbal. Available at: https://reports.galapagos.org/english/2019/6/29/women-inspiring-change-leadership-for-a-plastic-free-culture-in-san-cristbal/

Louv, R. (2005). *Last Child in the Woods: Saving our Children from Nature-Deficit Disorder*. California: Algonquin Books.

McCrory, P. (2021). *Hook Your Audience*. Belfast: Hook Training Ltd.

Milne, A. A. (1998). *Pooh invents a new game*. Massachusetts: Dutton Children's Books.

Natural History Museum (n.d.). Identify nature. Available at: https://www.nhm.ac.uk/take-part/identify-nature.html

Olusoga, D. (2023). Children's Media Conference, Opening Keynote. Available at: https://www.youtube.com/watch?v=mxKb1OXfS3w

Pathmanathan, S. (n.d.). Online resources for *A Creative Approach to Teaching Science Outdoors*. Available at: https://www.saipathmanathan.com/ScienceOutdoors

Plantlife (n.d.). Wildflower ID Guide: A guide to identification. Available at: https://www.plantlife.org.uk/wp-content/uploads/2023/12/WEB-Plantlife-Wild-Flowers-Count-ID-Wildflowers.pdf

Pritchard, M. (2018). 'Unleashing wonder and mystery in the classroom', in Billingsley, B., Abedin, M. and Chappell, K. (eds.) *A Teacher's Guide to Science and Religion in the Classroom*. London: Routledge.

Royal College of Pathologists (2016). The low allergy garden. Available at: https://www.rcpath.org/static/4a5e9fe8-bc2e-4097-a4f63a6ec116e1c4/Chelsea-Flower-Show-Leaflet-2016.pdf

Royal Horticultural Society (2024). Potentially harmful garden plants. Available at: https://www.rhs.org.uk/prevention-protection/potentially-harmful-garden-plants

Royal Society for the Protection of Birds Big Schools Bird Watch resources, Available at: https://www.rspb.org.uk/whats-happening/get-ready-for-big-schools-birdwatch/resources

Wildlife Trusts (n.d.) 'Bringing wildlife back on land'. Available at: https://www.wildlifetrusts.org/on-land

Index

acids 32–4, 86
alkalis 31–4, 86
allergies 4
A-maze-ing potatoes activity 52–3
Audio trails activity 128–30

bees 37, 59, 81 97–100, 106
beetle bucket 101–2
Berry nice activity 93–6
Big freeze activity 30–1
Bioblitz investigation activity 57–60
biodiversity 49, 57, 82–5, 125
birdfeeders
    natural 49
    loo roll 100–1
birdwatching 49
bridges, building 15–17
Bring in the bees activity 97–100

Can weeds help us? activity 105–8
cardboard hedgehog homes 104
Changing colours activity 31–4
chemical change 28–9
Circle of influence activity 130–2
climate change 31, 114, 117, 130–2
colour vision 70
compost 5–6, 75, 80, 83–84, 91, 93
cuttings and bulbs, growing plants from 96

density 21
diversity natives, teaching 7
dyes, natural 85–7

ears, and hearing 36, 76–7
ecosystems 57, 128
eco washing-up liquid 6, 19–20, 32, 108, 111
environmental friendliness 5–6
evaporation 22–3

fashion accessories 123–5
Feather forecast activity 26–8
feather paintbrushes 87
fertilisers, natural 109–10
flowers
    decorating bakes with 82
    edible 81–2
    PH indicators 32
    pollination 97–100, 106
    sunflower lifecycles 47
    wildflowers 85
food chains 47, 49, 105
food security 52
food waste 52, 93, 96
force 16, 20, 34, 38, 64, 68
friction 37–8

Game-changer activity 63–5
Get over it activity 15–17
gravity 34
Guess who? activity 42–4

habitats 55, 57, 59–60, 100, 104, 125
hearing process 35, 36–7
Heat is on activity 24–6
hedgehog habitats 104
Hole illusion activity 68–70
human impact on nature and biodiversity
        125–8

Ice to see you activity 115–17
ice-water transition 30
illusions 68–70
Incredible edibles activity 80–2
infusion 34
insects 59–60, 81, 97–100, 103, 106, 107, 110
insulation 26, 27–8
I Spy game 72

kokedama hanging basket 75

law of motion 15–16
Leaf me to race activity 19–21
leaf printing 87–8
leafy finger 42
learning cycle of wonder 1
leftover food 95
Let's pretend activity 70–2
lichen 54–5
ligaments 41, 77
light energy 24–5, 39
light properties and vision 68–9
loo-roll bird feeders 100–1
Louv, Richard, Nature Deficit Disorder 2

Magnus effect 65
Makes a lot of scents activity 78–9
Making a splash activity 65–6
Making nettle cordage activity 18
Marangoni effect 20
McCrory, Dr Paul, *Hook Your Audience* 1
measuring and counting activity 50–2
memories, and smells 78
memory activity 72–4
microplastics 118–19, 121–2, 124
mini insect hotels 102–3
moss 54–6, 75
movement, physics of 37, 63
Music to my ears activity 76–8

natural
    items 6
    manufacturing toy activity 121–3
    pest control 78–9
    rope making 17–19
Nature-Deficit Disorder 2
nest-building 26
nettle cordage making 18

observing nature 42–4
outdoor space limitations 5

Paint with nature activity 86–8
paper tape, recycled 6, 52, 56, 87, 102, 105
pesticides 79
pests 108–11

pH indicators 31
physical change 28–9
physics 16, 26, 63–4
Picking straws activity 119–21
plant pots, recycled 6, 45–6
plants
    exploration of 44–7
    growing food 93
    growth and reproduction 80–2, 105–8
Plants vs. pests activity 108–11
plastic crisis 118–23
pollination 97–100, 106
Poohsticks activity 66–8
Pritchard, Matt, 'learning cycle of wonder' 1

Rain savers activity 114–15
rainwater, collected 6
Reduce; reuse; recycle activity 91–3
refraction 40
Remember, remember activity 72–4
rope making, natural 17–19
runners, growing plants from 96

safety 4–5
scraps, growing food from 95
seeds
    comparing 96
    growing seedlings 81
    production 47–50
    seed balls 83
    seed-counting challenge 48
    seed postcards 85
Seed-sational activity 82–5
Seeds of time activity 44–7
sensitivities, consideration of 4
shadow creatures 40
Shadows and light activity 39–40
smells 78–9
soil 74–5
Sound it out activity 35–7
sounds 35–7, 76–8, 128–30
Sow your spice cupboard activity 84–5
special educational needs and disabilities (SEND) 2, 4
Spin me right 'round activity 37–9
sports 63–4

storytelling, and memory 73, 129
strawberries, growing 94–5
Sum it up activity 50–2
Sunflower power activity 47–50
surface tension 19–21, 65–6

Tendon loving care activity 41–2
terrariums 55–6
That sinking feeling activity 21–2
thinking like scientists 7
Time for a change activity 28–9
Tiny plastic everywhere activity 118–19
Toppling towers activity 34–5

vision 68–70

water
   cycle 22–4
   ice-water transition 30
   properties 19–20, 65, 66–8
   rainwater harvesting 114–15
Water day activity 22–4
Wear on Earth activity 123–5
weather, consideration of 5
Weave got strength activity 17–19
What on earth? activity 74–5
What was here before us? activity 125–8
Wildlife needs you activity 100–5
wildlife sounds 128–30
Wonderful world of worms activity 111–13

You're the lichen to my moss activity 54–6

Notes

These extra blank pages are for you to jot ideas down or even sketch something that you would like to show your group while you're all outside.

Notes

Notes

Notes

Notes

Notes

Notes

Notes

Notes

Notes